Action Learning and Action Research Journal

Vol 30 No 2 December 2024

Action Learning, Action Research Association Ltd (and its predecessors) has published the ALAR Journal since 1996.

Managing Editor: Dr Yedida Bessemer

Issue Editor: Dr Yedida Bessemer

Global Strategic Publications Editorial Board:
Prof John Andersen, Roskilde University, Denmark
Dr Azril Bacal, University of Uppsala, Sweden
Dr Christina Marouli, The American College of Greece, Greece
Riripeti Reedy, Ngati Porou, Director, Maitai Group Ltd, New Zealand

Editorial inquiries:
The Editor, *ALAR Journal*
Action Learning, Action Research Association Ltd
PO Box 162, Greenslopes, Qld 4120 Australia

editor@alarassociation.org

ISSN 1326-964X (Print)   ISSN 2206-611X (Online)

The Action Learning and Action Research Journal is listed in:

- Australian Research Council – *Excellence in Research for Australia (ERA) 2018 Journal List*
- Australian Business Deans Council - *2019 ABDC Journal Quality List*
- Norwegian Directorate for Higher Education and Skills - *Norwegian Register for Scientific Journals, Series and Publishers*

Editorial Advisory Board

Prof John Andersen	Denmark
Dr Rajiv George Aricat	India
Dr Azril Bacal Roji	Sweden / Chile
Dr Yedida Bessemer	USA / Israel
Dr Gina Blackberry	Australia
Colin Bradley	Australia
Dr Deeanna Burleson	USA
Dr Daniela Cialfi	Italy
Dr Ross Colliver	Australia
Mr Andrew Cook	Australia
Dr Philip Crane	Australia
Dr Bob Dick	Australia
Dr Kathryn Epstein	USA
Dr Terrance Fernsler	USA
Dr Susan Goff	Australia
Assoc. Prof. Marina Harvey	Australia
Dr Geof Hill	Australia
Ms Eimear Holland	Ireland
Ms Jane Holloway	Australia
Dr Magnus Hoppe	Sweden
Dr Ernest Hughes	USA
Dr Marie Huxtable	UK
Dr Edward Hyatt	USA
Dr Brian Jennings	Ghana
Dr Diane Kalendra	Australia
Prof. Vasudha Kamat	India
Prof. Nene Ernest Khalema	South Africa
Dr Elyssabeth Leigh	Australia
Dr Ashnie Mahadew	South Africa
Dr Tome Mapotse	South Africa
Prof Christina Marouli	Greece
Dr John Molineux	Australia
Dr Sumesh Nair	Australia

Assoc Prof Martha Elena Núñez-López	Mexico
Ms Margaret O'Connell	Australia
Dr Lizana Oberholzer	UK
Prof Akihiro Ogawa	Australia
Dr Chin Lye Ooi	Malaysia
Dr Elizabeth Orr	Australia
Dr Paul Pettigrew	UK
Dr Eileen Piggot-Irvine	New Zealand
Joe Poh	Malaysia
Ms Riripeti Reedy	New Zealand
Dr Akihiro Saito	Japan
Prof Shankar Sankaran	Australia
Assoc. Prof. Sandro Serpa	Portugal
Andrew Sporle	New Zealand
Prof Emmanuel Tetteh	USA
Dr Abbie Victoria Trott	Australia
Prof Jack Whitehead	UK
Assoc Prof Hilary Whitehouse	Australia

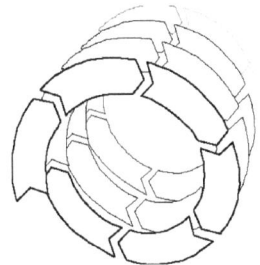

ALAR Journal

Volume 30 No 2
December 2024

ISSN 1326-964X (Print)
ISSN 2206-611X (Online)

CONTENTS

Editorial *Editor*	7
Leadership in action learning: Two case studies *Terrence Fernsler*	11
Engendering customer care and complaints handling in Government real estate companies in the Caribbean: change from below through action research *Erica Prentice and Ali Rostron*	49
"Hunchifactuality": Identifying and alleviating bias with pragmatic action research *Jack Brady*	83
Book Review – *A 101 Action Research Guide for Beginners* *Yedida Bessemer*	114

Membership information and article submissions	117

© 2024. Action Learning, Action Research Association Ltd and the author(s) jointly hold the copyright of *ALAR Journal* articles.

Editorial

Greetings,

The field of action research continues to evolve and offers various approaches to understanding and addressing real-world challenges. This *ALARj* issue includes three articles and a book review highlighting a significant link between theoretical frameworks and practical applications in action research. The first article is Leadership in Action Learning: Two Case Studies by Terrence Fernsler. The second article, Engendering Customer Care and Complaints Handling in Government Real Estate Companies in the Caribbean: change from Below through Action Research is by Erica Prentice and Ali Rostron. In the third article, "Hunchifactuality," Jack Brady identifies and alleviates bias with pragmatic action research. The fourth piece reviews the book *A 101 Action Research Guide for Beginners (Ahmed, 2024)*. The articles and book linked theoretical frameworks and practical applications in action research.

In the first article, Fernsler explores Action Learning and Complexity Leadership Theory in nonprofit organizations and shows how theoretical frameworks can illuminate leadership practices in dynamic environments. Fernsler's examination of the two case studies reveals that the characteristics of Action Learning—including acceptance of complexity, collective identity, and continuous reflection—naturally align with Complexity Leadership Theory, offering a fresh perspective on leadership in adaptive systems. Fernsler concluded,

> These two cases demonstrate that effective leadership in Action Learning environments is different from traditional perspectives, in that it is more distributed and not resting in one particular "heroic" individual (p. 44).

Similar to the first article, the second article focused on organizational change. Prentice and Rostron's study of customer relationship management in a Caribbean public sector enterprise provides a compelling example of insider action research in practice. Their work highlights how bottom-up change initiatives can succeed even without top management support, demonstrating the transformative potential of participatory research approaches. As indicated in the article,

> ...the lead author created meaningful change within her organization despite the lack of top management support. The intervention challenged the policies and procedures of the company and drove a change through co-opting staff who also sought to see change themselves and to be part of it (p. 76).

The authors' focus on employee empowerment and organizational transformation offers valuable insights into the practical application of action research principles in challenging institutional contexts.

In the third article, Brady wrote a reflective piece on pragmatic action research in studying Australian political comedy and introduced the novel concept of "hunchifactuality." He encourages researchers to value their experiential insights while maintaining awareness of potential biases. Brady asserted,

> A pragmatic AR approach, focused on how comedians were organized relative to what was important to them, meant further centering comedian experiences, processes, and logic, rather than the imposition of methods upon participants (p. 108).

His candid examination of researcher positionality and participant recruitment challenges speaks to the ongoing evolution of action research methodology and the importance of adaptability in research design.

The last piece of this issue is a book review of *A 101 Action Research Guide for Beginners* (Ahmed, 2024), which provides a structured approach to understanding and implementing action research for novice researchers, particularly in STEM education. Ahmed argued that

> Teaching practice is a spectrum. By learning the foundations of each theory teachers/ lecturers can pick and choose the level and degree to which it permeates into their teaching delivery, and on how they can affect action research projects (p.5).

The book demystified research terminology and offered concrete examples to help educators overcome challenges and improve their practice using action research.

All four pieces demonstrate the transformative potential of action research across diverse contexts, from nonprofit organizations to public sector enterprises and grassroots political movements. They all strive to navigate complexity and foster collaborative problem-solving. Whether addressing leadership in nonprofit organizations, improving customer care in state enterprises, or exploring political expression in the comedy scene, the common thread is the transformative power of collective action and reflective practice. This theme resonates strongly in Saba Ahmed's *A 101 Action Research Guide for Beginners*, which provides a roadmap for educators and practitioners to engage in systematic inquiry and evidence-based improvement. The guide's practical approach to explaining complex research concepts complements the methodological insights offered by Brady's work, while its focus on quality assurance and systematic implementation resonates with Prentice and Rostron's emphasis on organizational change. Furthermore, Ahmed's integration of national and international teaching frameworks provides a structured context for applying the complex theoretical perspectives discussed in Fernsler's article.

The collective understandings from these works highlight actionable pathways for fostering leadership, collaboration, and reflective inquiry across varied contexts. For practitioners, they emphasize the importance of embracing complexity and engaging stakeholders as co-creators of knowledge. They also advocate for iterative, participatory approaches that balance theories with practical relevance. The four works included in this issue demonstrate the ongoing growth of action research as a field that continues to bridge theory and practice in meaningful ways. From Fernsler's theoretical synthesis to Brady's methodological innovations and from Prentice and Rostron's practical application to Ahmed's comprehensive guide, we see the emergence of a more adaptive approach to action research.

Let's encourage readers to engage deeply with these works, considering how their insights might inform their research practices while fostering a culture of inquiry and innovation and contributing to the field's ongoing development. As action research evolves, integrating theoretical understanding with practical application remains vital for addressing complex social and organizational challenges.

To Lifelong Learning and to a Happy New Year,

Dr. Yedida Bessemer

Leadership in action learning: Two case studies
Terrence Fernsler

Abstract

Action Learning was developed in response to complex social environments to involve those most affected by change. It is especially well suited for the dynamic environment of the nonprofit sector which, based primarily in a relationship orientation more than a task orientation, is often dynamic and unpredictable. Shared leadership in Action Learning means operating in complex adaptive systems.

Complexity Leaderships Theory is a model of leading in organizations requiring adaptiveness, especially on an ongoing basis. It guides organizations that adopt complexity in their operating systems.

The two case studies of organizations presented in this article demonstrate the characteristics of Action Learning and how leadership was practiced during dramatic changes, using Complexity Leadership Theory as the basis. Many of the characteristics of Complexity Leadership Theory are applicable in Action Leaning settings, as demonstrated in this study.

Key words: Action learning, complexity leadership theory, dynamic environments, nonprofits

What is known about the topic?
Action Learning is a response to complex social environments to include those most effected by change or desiring to create change.
What does this paper add?
This paper explores how leadership in complex organizational environments was exhibited in two cases of organizations that transformed to Action Learning practice.
Who will benefit from its content?
Researchers and practitioners seeking ways to be more inclusive of lived experience can benefit from the examples of how the organizations in these cases adapted leadership styles.
What is the relevance to AL and AR scholars and practitioners?
We can learn how Complexity Leadership Theory is applicable in Action Learning settings.

Received   September 2023   Reviewed   August 2024   Published   December 2024

Introduction

Action Learning was first developed by Revans (1982) in the 1980s as a response to managing complex social environments. It takes a holistic approach to continually learning about and learning to improve social conditions. It is not neutral; it is intended to benefit all in a community, organization or team by attaining the highest human potential. It does this by involving the entire group's knowledge in decision-making and building structures to avoid exploitative practices and processes of people. While there has been little literature regarding leadership within Action Learning, we can learn much from descriptions of Action Learning.

Action Learning: A Process in Complex Adaptive Systems

Action Learning recognizes that social problems are interconnected and require action at a systems level involving multiple projects. While traditional strategies tend to offer clear, specific, and measurable outcomes that are achieved through processes detailed in linear logical models, such demands for pre-planned specificity do not work well in conditions of high uncertainty, turbulence, and emergence. Ongoing, interactive evaluation is more useful in social systems that are inherently dynamic and complex. Observations are needed from multiple participants collaborating while aware of what the environment is doing. By focusing on adaptive learning, Action Learning is a process that supports innovation in complex adaptive social systems. Regarding nonprofit organizations through the lens of complexity is valuable as a framework for making sense of and adapting to an environment. Social innovators (Patton, 2016) adapt programs to new contexts, catalyze systems change, and improvise rapid responses. Leadership in Action Learning involves facilitating these dimensions as described in Table 1.

Action Learning Characteristic	Source(s)
Acceptance of complexity	Pedlar, Burgoyne & Brook (2005)
Collective identity within systems (internal)	Revans (1982)
Continual learning through reflection on actions	Revans (1982), Garrett (1983)
Connectedness (awareness of place in the environment)	Revans (1982)
Creativity	Garrett (1983)
Credibility by being grounded in reality	Revans (1982)
Critical perspective catalyzes change	Revans (1982), Garrett (1983)
Emergence	Pedlar, Burgoyne & Brook (2005)
Sensemaking	Revans (1982), Garrett (1983)
Stewardship/ownership by community	Garrett (1983); Pedlar, Burgoyne & Brook (2005)

Table 1. Action Learning characteristics and sources found

Action Learning is designed to elicit knowledge that helps to resolve problems regarding fundamental issues (Pedlar, Burgoyne & Brook, 2005). It involves many people in the group learning from each other (Revans, 1982), identifying opportunity by expanding the logical procedure of rationality through the feedback of multiple individuals (Garrett, 1983).

While Pedler, Burgoyne & Brook (2005) claim that interest in Action Learning has been strongest among management development practitioners, and there is literature about its use in education (Kember, 2000; Lizzio & Wilson, 2004; McGill & Beaty, 2001; Zuber-Skerritt, 1993), Action Learning is particularly relevant to nonprofit organizations because of their identification as complex adaptive systems within complex adaptive systems.

Action Learning is a lifelong group learning process involving feedback loops and continuous improvement (Garratt, 1983) based on each participant's knowledge and willingness to lead. Action Learning requires action as the basis for learning through collective reflection, critical thinking, testing and re-testing, and organizational as well as personal development. Continual testing and adaptation is necessary in building knowledge (Pedlar, Burgoyne & Brook, 2005).

Collective understanding facilitates learning and resultant action on seemingly intractable issues by the whole group, rather than a teacher, trainer, or other expert (Pedlar, Burgoyne & Brook, 2005). It relies on continuous learning as the actions create change. Action Learning is given to those who have ownership of the problem and must live with the solution (Garrett, 1983). This complex set of participants in complex environments makes it ideal to practice within complex adaptive systems.

Action learning is participatory, involving feedback loops and continuous improvement (Garratt, 1983). It entails honest assessment and reflection, risk in taking shared action from critical thought, and trust in peers' diverse perspectives (Pedler & Burgoyne, 2015). It is a social process in which team members learn from each other (Revans, 1982). In such a complex, dynamic environment, what does leadership actually look like in action learning?

While there has been little literature regarding leadership within Action Learning, we can learn much from the descriptions of Action Learning. It may be impractical to expect any one individual to have the knowledge and ability to catalyze or coordinate all these dimensions, so leadership is necessarily distributed. Individuals may move into and out of leadership roles as needed according to the needs of the group and abilities of individuals, with the entire group monitoring themselves. This is an environment of complex leadership.

The study of leadership in organizations typically assumes leaders are individuals in a hierarchy who take an organization through a linear process to accurately predict a path toward accomplishing an organizational mission, eliminating or deflecting any ambiguity that characterizes much of operating in complex adaptive systems through interventions and control behaviors (Stacey, 1992; Wheatley, 1999).

Research Question

Complex adaptive systems share the common attributes of adaptiveness, interdependence, overlap, and coevolution (Foster, 2005). Organizations operating in complex systems take on properties and structures that are unexpected (McKelvey & Lichtenstein, 2007) because people and groups interact producing perpetual novelty. This document presents two case studies in which leadership in complex adaptive systems is based on the work of complexity leadership scholars such as Marion & Uhl-Bien (2002), Lichtenstein et al. (2006), Uhl-Bien, Marion & McKelvey (2007), and Hazy & Uhl-Bien (2012). The cases are observations of organizations that underwent rapid and successful change. They provide a rare opportunity to closely observe the emergence of leadership in a dynamic organization by continually evaluating. The research question driving this study was *what characteristics does leadership actually take in an action learning system involving complex environments?*

The two cases in this study explore how that was applied. The cases rely on a qualitative theory development approach (Miles & Huberman, 1994; Yin, 2003) and finds support for Marion & Uhl-Bien's (2002) concept that leaders in complex adaptive systems *enable* rather than *control or manage* tasks leading to desirable futures. They identify the leadership mechanisms that were used and specific actions taken to learn and adapt in a complex learning environment. The findings support that leadership in Action Learning closely follows the characteristics of Complexity Leadership Theory (Hazy & Uhl-Bien, 2002; Lichtenstein, et al., 2006; McKelvey & Lichtenstein, 2007; Marion & Uhl-Bien, 2002).

Literature review

To study leadership in Action Learning, it is first necessary to understand what leadership is in complex, adaptive organizations. Traditionally, leadership was the domain of individuals in an organization. Collins (2001) argued that organizational greatness is due to one fundamental ingredient: leaders. In book after book, Kotter (1985, 1990, 1996) argued it is leaders who make organizational transformation happen by directing change. However, as early as 1978, Kerr & Jermier (1978) minimized the significance of leadership by identifying substitutes for the individual-centered approach.

The emerging view of organizations as complex adaptive systems operating in dynamic environments challenges the fundamental premise of what leadership is. The traditional view of leadership is based on the idea that the world is knowable as a kind of complicated mechanical system in which discernable forces and basic laws of motion operate (Capra, 1996). In this view, organizations consist of highly prescribed rule sets, formalized control, and hierarchical authority structures that simplify ongoing operations and lead to well-defined and predictable responses to a slowly-evolving world. Organizations seek order and stability by reducing complexity through codification (Boisot & Child, 1999), solving problems through reductionist thinking (Ashmos, et al., 2002), and engaging in often complicated, yet linear, planning

(Wheatley, 1999). From this perspective, leaders try to control the future by acting to reduce complexity and uncertainty establishing followers and directing them towards highly prescribed states. While the study of leadership has been an important part of traditional organizational science for decades, it has disappointed many practitioners in the nonprofit sector because the proliferation of leadership theories has little application in the complex environments of constant change and overlap of issues in which many nonprofit organizations find themselves, especially in environments that are compelling social movements that involves constant change and overlapping issues.

Complex adaptive systems

Increasingly, linear models proved to be ineffective in capturing the complex and emergent nature of most observed phenomenon (Kauffman, 1993; Prigogine, 1997). In nature, randomness balances with determinism; self-regulation in complex living systems continually adjusts probabilities of where a system should move, what actions members should take, and, as a result, how deeply to explore particular pathways within networks (Mitchell, 2009). When strategizing, humans are not limited to one direction. As Schwartz (1991) indicates, the creative fringe, where adaptive behaviors emerge, can be important to planning, especially in response to driving forces in their environment.

Niklas Luhmann (1995) developed the concept of living social systems in detail, identifying the social processes of the living system network as processes of communications. Since these processes take place in social domains, system boundaries are not physical boundaries, but those set by such things as expectations, confidentiality and loyalty. Social systems are continually maintained and renegotiated through relationships.

Organizations exist in conditions of instability, and as they move further away from equilibrium towards instability, they are capable of highly complex behavior (Anderson, 1999; McKelvey, 2001; Stacey, 1992; Wheatley, 1999). The more traditional, mechanistic view of organizations are not especially workable in many real situations because they over-simplify models of organizational theory (Marion & Uhl-Bien, 2002).

Complex systems are characterized as non-linear because the components that comprise them are constantly interacting with each other through a web of feedback loops (Anderson, 1999; Stacey, 1995). A small fluctuation in one small part of a system could trigger unexpected, perhaps profound and unpredictable changes to other parts of the system, near in time or distant.

Maguire & McKelvey (1999) argue that when organizations move away from stability and into the complex, adaptive tensions give rise to emergent self-organization. Indeed, many argue that it is only as organizations move into disequilibrium that emergent ideas become possible, giving rise to innovation and creativity (Anderson, 1999; Chiles, Meyer & Hench, 2004; McKelvey, 1999). This presents challenges to the way of thinking about leadership (Marion & Uhl-Bien, 2002).

Leadership in Complex Systems

From a complex adaptive systems perspective, leaders do not direct change or control future outcomes, as traditional leadership prescribes. Leaders in complex systems require models for problem solving performed through the relationships in social networks. Complexity Leadership Theory (CLT) models (Hazy & Uhl-Bien, 2012; Lichtenstein et al. 2006; Marion & Uhl-Bien, 2002; Uhl-Bien, Marion & McKelvey, 2007) describe leadership characteristics in complex adaptive systems. Effective leadership in these conditions is not so much about structure as about the interdependent agency within groups. CLT explores how organizations can enable adaptive responses to challenges through network-based problem solving. It offers tools for organizations and subsystems dealing with rapidly changing, complex problems. Effective leaders recognize the importance of interactions, interdependence, and unpredictability among group members (Marion & Uhl-Bien, 2002). Leadership in complexity allows relationships to emerge through the engagement of non-linear processes (Regine & Lewin, 2000). These interactions help facilitate what Marion & Uhl-Bien (2002) describe as the emergence of a common or shared understanding of the system. They help organizational participants make sense out of what is happening. In other words, leadership in complexity enables emergence by participants becoming catalysts for actions (Holland, 1995; Marion & Uhl-Bien, 2002), to enable or speed up specific behaviors by directing attention to what is important to a group's purpose.

Leadership Characteristics in Complexity Leadership Theory

Multiple, simultaneous collaborations with flexible planning result in a highly dynamic, highly-networked environment in which to operate. A critical perspective interprets rather than creates change (Plowman et al., 2007). System component knowledge resides in multiple individuals within an organization but information is shared openly.

Lichtenstein et al. (2006) suggest that a complexity-based perspective deters leadership from resting within one person, but in 'an interactive dynamic within which any particular person will participate as a leader or follower at different times and for different purposes' (p. 3) due to the emergent nature of events. Hazy and Uhl-Bien's (2012) unifying function of complexity leadership theory promotes collective identities to coalesce this leadership role. Complex adaptive systems are grounded in reality. The ability to maneuver in larger systems requires collective expertise, knowledge, and the ability to manage relationships (Gamble, 2008). Leaders cannot control the future because in complex adaptive systems, unpredictable dynamics and diverse participants determine conditions. Plowman et al. (2007) found effective groups enabled such emergent futures through disrupting behaviors that surfaced conflict or tension and created uncertainty. Marion & Uhl-Bien (2002) state that it is important that complexity be recognized and accepted, and even, as Alexander (1998) would describe it, exploited.

Leadership in complex adaptive systems responds to changing constraints in the environment partially through internal collaboration (Hazy & Uhl-Bien, 2012) because problem solving is performed by appropriately structured social networks evaluating feedback loops rather than through highly coordinated centralized authorities (Uhl-Bien, Marion &McKelvey, 2007). Hazy & Uhl-Bien (2012) assert that the 'acquisition of leadership skills by individuals is the result of social learning of the meta-capability within organizations' (p. 22). Adaptation 'engages individuals and organizations in search, experimentation, and variation to enhance creativity and learning' (Hazy & Uhl-Bien, 2012, p. 25). Continual learning and adaptation, then, is required in complex adaptive systems.

Plowman et al. (2007) found that leaders in complex adaptive systems encouraged innovation; they challenged organization members to come up with ideas and investigate them. Hazy & Uhl-Bien (2012) explain that adaptations elicit innovations that can be exploited to the benefit of the organization; creativity and innovation are important in complex systems to adapting procedures to changing circumstances.

There is much value in understanding and incorporating cultural attitudes. The value of organizational cultural awareness within a network of organizations (Schein, 2017) can be equally important. Alaimo (2008) encourages cultural awareness and belonging for all stakeholders internal and external to the group to consider holistic perspectives in effective leadership.

Plowman et al. (2007) touch on sensemaking as important in Complexity Leadership Theory. The many interacting and overlapping variables of complex adaptive systems can easily become confusing. Finding some way for participants to make sense of all these interactions, particularly when working on multiple issues, is often necessary to understand the weblike pattern and constant structural changes within the system.

Stewardship means being in service to participants while they are equally participating—lived/living experiences increase investment into learning through action. Service to the community is emphasized by Dozois, Langlois & Blanchet-Cohen (2010).

Table 2. below summarizes the characteristics of leadership identified in Complexity Leadership and the research in which they were identified.

Complexity Leadership Characteristic	Explanation and source(s)
Acceptance of complexity	Enabling emergence through disrupting behaviors that surface conflict or tension and create uncertainty because futures cannot be controlled (Marion & Uhl-Bien, 2002; Plowman et al., 2007)
Collective identity connected within systems	An interactive dynamic within which any particular person will participate as a leader or follower at different times and for different purposes (Lichtenstein, et al. 2006). Leadership in complex adaptive systems responds to changing constraints in the environment partially through collaboration (Hazy & Uhl-Bien, 2012)
Continual learning and adaptation	Continual learning and adaptation (Hazy & Uhl-Bien, 2012)
Creativity	Adaptations elicit innovations and creative responses (Hazy & Uhl-Bien, 2012; Plowman et al., 2007)
Credibility	Understanding organizational cultural attitudes (Alaimo, 2008; Schein, 2017)
Critical perspective catalyzes change through emergence	Interpreting rather than creating change (Plowman, et al., 2007) and creating transformational change in the sense of changing the abilities of the organization and its participants and reflections of actions taken (Gamble, 2008)

Complexity Leadership Characteristic	Explanation and source(s)
Emergence	Descriptions through tensions (Plowman et al., 2007)
Sensemaking	Helping the organization to break down what it is, how to strategize in a way that makes sense for the long-term (Plowman et al., 2007)
Stewardship	Being in service to the process and its participants all of whom are equally participating (Dozois, Lanlois, & Blanchet-Cohen, 2010)
Systemic	The value of understanding and incorporating attitudes and learning; the value from a network of organizations (Alaimo, 2008; Schein, 2017)

Table 2. Complexity Leadership characteristics

Methodology

This study relies on an inductive approach, consistent with methodology used in similar research (Eisenhardt, 1989; Isabella, 1990). It is a critical auto-ethnology case study with a mix of narrative inquiry. It uses Complexity Leadership Theory as the foundation of leadership in complex adaptive systems. Alexander (1998) used a qualitative approach to observe the interactions and behaviors that characterize complex adaptive system leadership in a startup nonprofit organization exploiting complexity. The study considers two distinct organizations operating in a complex adaptive system as they progressed through continuous, radical change. Leadership characteristics are based on the dimensions of leadership in complex adaptive systems found by Hazy & Uhl-Bien (2012), Lichtenstein eta al. (2006), McKelvey & Lichtenstein (2007), and Marion & Uhl-Bien (2002).

The narrative in this study revolves around the activities of its author. Attribution bias is mitigated in this case through organizational documents, including board of directors and committee meeting minutes. Interviews of key stakeholders, including board members and, in the case of Columbia-Pacific RC&EDD, a knowledgeable staff participant, to gather additional data were conducted to triangulate the researcher's auto-ethnography and written records, as suggested by Merriam & Tisdell (2016).

Data collection

Data came from three sources: (1) observation by the researcher, (2) open-ended interviews of three former board of director members who also served on the steering committee in Habitat for Humanity of Grays Harbor, and (3) secondary sources. In the Columbia-Pacific RC&EDD case, data came from (1) researcher observations, (2) open-ended interviews of two Governing Council members, a former Governing Council and two interns for Columbia-Pacific RD&EDD, and (3) secondary sources. The researcher was deeply immersed in the process and operations of both organizations. The researcher's role was complete participant, as there was no intention to use the activities for research purposes at the time of their occurrence. Official and unofficial documents of the organizations were utilized as secondary sources for these studies to further triangulate the findings. Access to many documents was provided, including annual reports and budgets, newsletters, reports to external funders and agencies, meeting minutes, and committee reports, correspondence (letters and email), grant awards, media reports and articles, and project award nominations.

Researcher observation represented the primary source of data. Being embedded in the organizations offered the opportunity to examine in fine-grained detail the leadership characteristics in changing organizations. Immediately after each interview of participants (which occurred years after the events described took place), the researcher added impressions, following Eisenhardt's (1989) rules by: (1) developing detailed interview notes within 24 hours, (2) including all data from the interview, and (3) concluding each set of interview notes with the researchers' overall impressions. Interviews were organized into three dimensions: respondent's background and their role and relationship to the organization; purpose, mission, and uniqueness of the organization and processes; and finally, challenges and opportunities facing the organization at the time.

Data analysis

The researcher created a narrative account of the impact that leadership had on the startup and growth of each organization and the impact the environment had on leadership. This analytic approach is appropriate for organizing longitudinal data, especially when based on a single case with abundant information (Langley, 1999). The narrative was developed based on the researcher's review, understanding, and text analyses of interviews, observations, and documents in an effort to make sense of the data (Miles & Huberman, 1994). Reviewing the story while returning to the literature on leadership and complexity science ultimately led to the framework used.

The researcher reviewed each transcript sentence by sentence and identified all notations associated with the overall theme of leadership. He then coded the notations into the Complexity Leadership Theory characteristics described above. The reporting includes only data that were substantiated across multiple information sources.

Findings

Findings from the study suggest that complexity leadership dimensions were key factors contributing to organizational growth. The study specifically examines the leadership behaviors within the organizations initiated from the interaction of individuals who served on the steering committee/board of directors for Habitat for Humanity of Grays Harbor and the Governing Council of Columbia-Pacific Resource Conservation and Economic Development Council (Columbia-Pacific RC&EDD), not from the direction of a single nominal leader.

Case 1: Habitat for Humanity of Grays Harbor

The success of Habitat for Humanity of Grays Harbor (HFHOGH) grew from the interactions of multiple stakeholders affected by housing decisions desiring to alleviate dilapidated housing in a low-income area. A steering committee formed to create a local affiliate of Habitat for Humanity International, not by directing change but by catalyzing participation. The Steering Committee, which later became the board of directors upon successfully affiliating, worked hard to be reflective of its constituents, in terms of ethnicity, gender representation, religious affiliation, and beneficiary representation. It adopted an organizational culture of openness, expressing and accepting opinions and looking out for and supporting service to all parts of its service area.

The Chair of the Steering Committee, who served as liaison with Habitat for Humanity International, would introduce ideas such as asking Care-A-Vanners (retirees traveling in recreational vehicles around the United States helping local Habitat for Humanity affiliates to build homes), hosting a Women's Build, or accepting the 21st Century Challenge (leading a strategy to eliminate all substandard housing in a service area) to the board, but allow the members to discuss and decide whether or not to adopt them. Learning was frequently discussed, including how to implement projects given limited financial resources and using volunteer resources. HFHOGH members reflected on challenges with each other and quickly learned from them. The Chair also learned who to turn to and created informal "response teams" when new issues arose, such as in-kind donations of real estate by banks and new neighbor concerns; the board learned who had the talent to handle challenges. By the organization's third year, the organization had completed two homes, had three other homes in different stages of progress simultaneously, and planned to have four the following year and five the year after that.

The Secretary of Habitat for Humanity of Grays Harbor often noted in the minutes that the board of directors came to consensus about decisions, whether emergent (such as the decision to sponsor a parade float that turned out to be a community favorite) or revealed as external threats (such as the neighbors who thought of Habitat for Humanity partner families as threats to the community) through discussion.

The collective identity of HFHOGH was promoted at the time of the formation of the Steering Committee—the task force that established procedures in order to meet the Habitat for Humanity International requirements for affiliation. The chairs of each of the newly-formed subcommittees had sufficient autonomy, based on their members' expertise, to review suggested policies and to revise them as needed while still meeting the criteria that Habitat for Humanity International set. When the Steering Committee transitioned to the board of directors, the Chair was asked to serve as its founding board chair, a vote of confidence in the organization's community identity. The committees, which had developed policies for the affiliation process were now given autonomy to implement them, but all recommendations were fully discussed and considered by the entire board of directors. Board members felt at ease to express differences with each other because they had accomplished so much together and had come to respect the perspectives of each member. One of the board members interviewed noted how decisions were introduced to the board as a whole after being considered by an appropriate committee and offered for discussion.

HFHOGH learned to be comfortable with complexity and ambiguity early on in the formation of the steering committee by taking on initiatives with unknown outcomes—such as beginning an affiliate. After two better-known community meeting members turned down the invitation to chair the Steering Committee, the participants asked a relatively unknown who was new to the community, but had some connections to Habitat for Humanity International, to chair the committee. There was also comfort with complexity when accepting the Twenty-first Century Challenge, knowing how much more networking and collaborating would be required in the community to accomplish the challenge: to lead in the development of a plan to eliminate all substandard housing in the county. That decision was made because the board members recognized they collectively had the community connections to catalyze community organizations and local government agencies, as noted in the board minutes.

HFHOGH had already connected with its community through multiple collaborations to publicize the organization and solicit contributions. HFHOGH began by cooperating with like-minded organizations rather than compete with them, respecting their expertise. Credibility with external stakeholders was evidenced in collaborations with many external organizations, such as building suppliers (which donated or provided materials at cost), and multiple congregations in the county. An interviewee who was a member of the board of directors confirmed that it was perhaps easier to develop social capital in a small, relatively isolated community.

Continual learning and adaptation became an important feature of leadership with HFHOGH. Board members began learning from each other and its own early efforts. For example, there were delays in completing the first home, despite having key resources available before even being affiliated and accepting applications for a partner family. Some of the obstacles were construction and land preparation issues, some were legal issues, and some delays were caused when trying to schedule the partner family to complete their required volunteer hours. HFHOGH sought the expertise of different knowledge bases and various experts for information on things such as sites for appropriate land use, legal concerns, involving social workers in family support and selection (especially when families had to be rejected), building codes and amenities to build into the home, and even getting the best from public relations. These were all coordinated collectively among board members (and others in committees) knowledgeable about all the committees' work.

Creativity is frequently difficult to define, especially with a Habitat for Humanity affiliate that had the knowledge of many other affiliates upon which to draw. Still, HFHOGH was innovative in the way it functioned collectively—rather than compartmentalizing—and by strategic flexibility. The organization found creative ways to find properties—its first six were all donated, including one from the County, which resisted the donation at first. Here again, having broad reach in a small, impoverished community helped trigger creative responses. The organization also maneuvered through other contributions; for example, on two occasions two different banks donated foreclosed houses to HFHOGH. One of the homes had a ready private buyer and was sold for an amount which gave HFHGOH enough cash to build almost two new Habitat homes. HFGOGH also worked with two foundations for the first collaborative initiative between them by jointly paying for the cost of a new home. The ability to build five homes as an all-volunteer organization was creative as well.

The organization understood the big picture was to provide decent affordable housing for all in the county, not just building homes, because of the social determinants of housing. The board of directors was blessed both with people who were willing to discuss ultimate goals (for example the board chair) and those able to strategize the incremental steps to accomplishing the goals (such as the retired building inspector who served on the board of directors) all while making sense of how to accomplish low-income housing development without using paid employees.

Empowering each other and the community with information about fulfilling needs and sharing resources, and persistence in obtaining support, demonstrated stewardship to the community, not just the organization. The monthly board of directors meetings encouraged ongoing feedback and evaluation, cultivating and stewarding relationships internally and externally. Flexibility for how goals were accomplished demonstrated a desire to find the best ways to work with the community. The board never seemed to lose sight of its service to the community—the desire to help as many families as possible, even starting a chapter to serve low-income families in a remote part of the county — which drove the rapid pace of growth.

These characteristics of Complexity Leadership Theory in Habitat for Humanity of Grays Harbor were driven by community members learning from each other to effectively improving the community in which they lived. Table 3 summarizes them.

Leadership dimension	Example in HFHOGH
Acceptance of complexity	Starting a Habitat for Humanity affiliate. Deciding to lead a strategy to eliminate all substandard housing in the county.
Collective identity connected within systems	Multiple examples include the relative autonomy of committees and the board coordination of their activities. Cultivating and stewarding volunteers and faith-based organizations. Agreeing to coordinate the Twenty-first Century Challenge.
Continual learning through adaptation	Surveying obtained properties, dealing with opposition in the community, improving the auction event, finding new ways to recruit market, such as the parade float and a variety of media tactics, better planning for construction.
Creativity	Aggressively soliciting in-kind donations, especially of real estate. Managing volunteer labor in all aspects of the operation.
Credibility	Vision and ability to create the organization in a low-income community. Accepting the 21st Century Challenge. Collaborating with like-minded nonprofit organizations and businesses.

Leadership dimension	Example in HFHOGH
Critical perspective catalyzes change through emergence	Bringing ideas to the steering committee and board of directors to let members decide to implement initiatives such as inviting Care-A-Vanners, a Women's Build, and accepting the Twenty-first Century Challenge. Utilizing expertise in law, family support, construction, finances, land use; collaborating and supporting each other.
Emergence	Unexpected issues arising with one of the neighbors. Property acquisitions.
Sensemaking	Seeing the big picture of eliminating substandard housing; building relationship to achieve organizational goals. Celebrating with the beneficiaries. Open communication and trust.
Stewardship	Allowing the board of directors to make decisions about initiatives; learning from the committees about how to fulfill needs and connecting resources; empowering families and volunteers; cross-communication and participation.
Systemic	Encouraging representation of diverse faiths; low-income and youth representation on the board of directors. Increased collaboration among members; learning about members' expertise and connecting at meetings; open communication leading to trust

Table 3. Leadership dimensions and examples in Habitat for Humanity of Grays Harbor case

Case 2: Columbia-Pacific RC&EDD Leadership Dimensions

Columbia-Pacific Resource Conservation & Economic Develop District (Columbia-Pacific RC&EDD) worked on conservation when it decided to expand services in its four-county, low-income area in rural western Washington state. The dramatic change in Columbia-Pacific RC&EDD resulted from the decision to exploit complexity rather than, as is traditionally taught and expected, deflecting it (Alexander, 1998). The organization transitioned over time from a one-issue (conservation) organization to taking on multiple projects using a variety of means and collaborations. Some of the collaborations involved the member organizations working together, sometimes with support from Columbia-Pacific RC&EDD resources, sometimes without its direct assistance. Many collaborations involved organizations and even networks of organizations external to the rural four-county District. The organization's reputation grew rapidly with Washington State agencies such as The State Historical Planning Committee for the Lewis and Clark Bicentennial and the Department of Community, Trade and Economic Development, federal agencies such as the Rural Advisory Committee for the Olympic National Forest, Rural Utilities Service, and other Department of Agriculture agencies, and the U. S. Economic Development Administration, and with private nonprofit organizations such as the National Training Center for Small Communities and the Washington State Small Business Incubation Association.

Many of the organization's initiatives had no formal strategic plans, but explored opportunities strategically learning by doing, reflecting, and acting. Multiple, simultaneous collaborations with flexible planning resulted in a highly dynamic, highly-networked environment in which to operate—a complex adaptive system operating within the geographically-based boundaries. A Council member remarked how representatives would be allowed to raise concerns affecting their communities and whether solutions using those resources or Columbia-Pacific RC&EDD's follow-up was needed.

Member organizations, initially consisting primarily of local government agencies and their representatives on the Governing Council, became more engaged in determining which initiatives the organization selected to work on. New members were invited to join the organization, hoping to make it more representative of the community, including two state legislators, private nonprofit organizations, and one private business. A number of stakeholders participated in leadership roles, but no one individual seemed to be directing the change. One of the federal Coordinators noted how representation on the Governing Council grew as new issues were considered and especially as they were accomplished. With increased recognition and successes, other member organizatons wanted to become part of Columbia-Pacific RC&EDD

The change emerged from ongoing interactions between participants, both internally and externally, learning and adapting together rather than relying on a single individual for direction. Leadership disrupted existing patterns of behavior by introducing characteristics of Action Learning. All acted interdependently when they took on new initiatives. The nominal leaders at Columbia-Pacific RC&EDD played a key role in the change that occurred, not by using legitimate power to specify or direct change but by creating conditions that allowed for the emergence of such change, including efforts to maintain distributed leadership.

Change was often introduced when staff and Governing Council members brought ideas back from conferences they attended on behalf of the organization. Conference attendees from Columbia-Pacific RC&EDD would report those initiatives used elsewhere that might fit needs and resources of the District and allow the full Governing Council to decide whether to implement similar projects in the District. Adaptations were frequently discussed, especially how to implement projects given limited financial resources. Sometimes this would mean member organizations would sponsor the initiative, such as when Shorebank Pacific, and later Coastal Community Action Program (both member organizations in Columbia-Pacific RC&EDD), sponsored programs to assist low-income workers that helped them acquire and maintain affordable transportation through the Wheels to Work program. The Wheels to Work program involved multiple participants, including previously independent, non-collaborative organizations, such as banks willing to offer low-interest loans to clients with the guarantee from Shorebank and reduced costs from automobile mechanics.

Sometimes it meant Columbia-Pacific RC&EDD found alternative means to conducting initiatives, such as when interns were trained to conduct a feasibility study for a virtual small business incubator rather than contracting outside consultants. Even interns became excited about their sense of belonging in an organization that was willing to include them in emergent solutions.

The collective identity of Columbia-Pacific RC&EDD was promoted by presenting all proposals to the Governing Council before strategizing and implementation would take place. Some collaborative initiatives, such as a telecommunications project, in which broadband was brought to nearly all customers in the District (and indeed, the entire West Coast of Washington state), utilized the expertise of individual member organizations (particularly public utility districts) under the auspices of Columbia-Pacific RC&EDD and brought together participants outside the District, both local agencies and governments, the state Community Trade and Economic Development department, and several U.S. Department of Agriculture agencies. This was intentional on the part of the Economic Development District Director, federal Coordinator, and Council Chair.

Council members would sometimes need to raise issues, such as finding clean water solutions at low or no cost for the entire District and found resources to help develop programs that became national models.

Other initiatives, such as the SenioRx program to offer affordable prescriptions medication to low-income elderly residents were piloted in one community using the pooled resources of Columbia-Pacific RC&EDD member organizations. Another collaboration with the State Historical Lewis and Clark Bicentennial Commission along with local governments in Oregon and Washington created an end-of-the-trail coalition near the mouth of the Columbia River. These regional collaborations strengthened ties with state and federal resource providers, allowing even more initiatives that benefitted the constituents. These connections were cultivated and stewarded by multiple members of the Governing Council. The members felt supported in their efforts to organize within their communities and pass lessons learned on to other representatives of the Governing Council in the District.

Columbia-Pacific RC&EDD displayed comfort with complexity by taking on initiatives with unknown outcomes, such as the Rural Communities Development Initiative, particularly a component involving listening sessions in eight rural communities in Grays Harbor County. The organization also cultivated and stewarded relationships with unknown consequences, including that with a newly-appointed Washington State Community, Trade and Economic Development Director. These relationships gained access to resources where they had not been attempted previously and served as a model for later efforts.

Even some of the intern hires had unknown outcomes, especially those positions tailored for specific interns, such as the legal intern who ended up working on nine projects over one summer, and his assistant, who had no job description other to aid and shadow the legal intern. A request was presented for the intern to work on projects and Council members responded with tasks to research revising city codes, human resource law on the high seas, marketing carbon credits, and more. The organization was willing to risk overcrowding the office space with interns and exploited the condition to catalyze high energy within the group, with interns affected most by this, expressing how the cramped quarters and sharing information fed into their learning for themselves and the organization.

Continual adaptation and learning is required in complex adaptive systems, and became an important feature of leadership for Columbia-Pacific RC&EDD. Member organizations and staff began learning from each other. Innovation, such as the virtual small business incubation project, a wastewater training program and the telecommunications programs helped the organization adjust and refocus efforts as new information would be obtained. The flexibility allowed by not developing rigid strategic plans for initiatives meant that projects were evaluated constantly by members of the community. Learning from these on-going evaluations allowed rapid and sometimes creative adaptation.

Columbia-Pacific RC&EDD utilized creative (at least by Columbia-Pacific RC&EDD standards) ways to meet old or difficult problems. A Landscape Management System (LMS) initiative to test the carbon market for small landowners and building a cooperative for them to go to scale were innovative methods of increasing income for small landowners. The wastewater treatment training initiative took a new approach to meeting clean water requirements that would not bankrupt rural communities. Unique solutions for providing broadband telecommunication to rural residents in different parts of the District were shared among members and organizations outside the District. These all served as creative response models, according to the CTED Director. Finally, when the organization could not afford high-priced consultants, it learned to use interns to conduct a feasibility study for a virtual small business incubator. It also explored ways to effect community development initiatives in low-income communities through supervising Americorps*VISTA members.

Member organizations learned to help each other maneuver through processes to resolve local concerns. This began at the monthly Governing Council meetings, with representatives of member organizations communicating with each other to learn and discuss more details of initiatives. Staff at Columbia-Pacific RC&EDD took the time to cultivate and steward relationships with prospective funders, and were willing to act as liaisons when necessary, to clarify funding agency and grantor desires and match them more effectively with local needs. In some instances, this took as much as three years, as in the cases of support for universal broadband telecommunications in the District, developing a wastewater treatment training pilot program, and the Rural

Community Development Initiative (RCDI). Credibility with external stakeholders was evidenced when these and other projects were fully-funded and when the CTED Director reassigned her staff, at Columbia-Pacific RC&EDD's request, who were delaying progress on the telecommunication and LMS initiatives. Funders and collaborators began approaching Columbia-Pacific RC&EDD through various representatives to the Governing Council.

Columbia-Pacific RC&EDD accepted adaptations to plans for providing broadband in different regions of the District to meet local situations. Columbia-Pacific RC&EDD also built upon the strong history of cooperatives in the Pacific Northwest to try to develop a new one for carbon sequestration credits, a novel concept at the time. The organization developed a precedent for making decisions collectively, and making time to consider dissension, getting to know each member organization's strengths and weaknesses (and their service areas' assets), cultivating mentors for specialized issues, and adapting to the strengths of all participants

Columbia-Pacific RC&EDD pulled on different knowledge bases, different programs, and different ideas as critical to learning. In most cases, local expertise, such as how to reach target audiences for SenioRx, what businesses could benefit from small business incubation services, or the inputs for determining wastewater treatment systems in particular communities was supplemented by technical expertise found outside the District.

The many interacting and overlapping variables of complex adaptive systems can easily become confusing. Finding some way for participants to make sense of all these interactions, particularly when working on multiple issues, is often necessary to understand the weblike pattern and constant structural changes within the system. At Columbia-Pacific RC&EDD, member organizations learned from each other the similarity of concerns across the District while simultaneously learning different approaches to address those concerns. They began to see economic development as inclusive of community development and conservation; recognizing these as interrelated made more sense.

Requiring the Governing Council itself to make decisions about whether to proceed with initiatives before staff plunged forward indicated a sense of service to the community, who the members of the Governing Council represented. Empowering each other with information about fulfilling needs and sharing sources of prospective support and persistence in obtaining that support, demonstrated stewardship to communities, which themselves tended to be under resourced. Its culture of sharing responsibilities demonstrated that client communities were more important than the reputation of Columbia-Pacific RC&EDD itself. The tailored programs of the wastewater treatment training program and the RCDI initiative showed the desire to build capacity rather than mold initiatives into pre-determined programs. The monthly Governing Council meetings encouraged ongoing debriefing and evaluation, cultivating and stewarding relationships internally and externally. Flexibility for how staff and interns accomplished goals demonstrated finding the best ways to help them serve the community.

The participants in this newly-acknowledged complex system destabilized, rather than stabilized, the organization, especially by shying from a structure to achieve a specific, pre-planned desired state. Participants in Columbia-Pacific RC&EDD encouraged the organization towards disequilibrium by introducing uncertainty and comfort with complexity, a state from which novelty could emerge. At the same time, participants also provided some order (sensemaking) by interpreting and giving meaning to the actions that emerged from the disequilibrium. Participants were swept up in behaviors of collective innovation as progress was made. By encouraging non-linear, non-compartmentalized interactions, participants encouraged each other and their organizations to be innovative rather than assume all the responsibility for innovative ideas.

Conveners of Columbia-Pacific RC&EDD played their role well, making sure ideas were introduced and discussed. These characteristics of Complexity Leadership Theory in Columbia-Pacific RC&EDD are summarized in Table 4.

Leadership dimension	Example
Acceptance of complexity	Cultivating and stewarding relationship with CTED director; Overcrowding of office with interns; multiple projects for legal intern; hiring interns with no known outcomes predicted; COG RCDI initiative, with unknown outcomes
Collective identity connected within systems	Multiple examples include: SeniorRx, Wheels to Work, Telecommunications initiative. Cultivating and stewarding relationships with EDA, USDA, Historical Commission, OR Lewis & Clark, CTED, Telecomm entities outside the District, RAC
Continual learning through reflection of actions	Ways to approach experts in feasibility study; learning to do a feasibility study; new approach to incubator; adapting Wheels to Work; adopting SenioRx; learning of alternative wastewater solutions; learning and connecting needs of various communities
Creativity	LMS proposals; NETCSC proposal; adaptive telecom proposals; interns to fulfill projects; VISTA program to initiate systemic program
Credibility	Community SWOT assessments and recruiting resources when necessary from outside agencies.
Critical perspective catalyzes change through emergence	Bringing ideas to the Governing Council to let members decide to implement initiatives such as Wheels to Work and SenioRx first; training interns to do a feasibility study

Leadership dimension	Example
Sensemaking	Learning from members of region-wide concerns; expanding economic development to include conservation and community development; taking on regional not community issues; adopting a holistic approach to programs
Stewardship	Allowing governing council to make decisions about initiatives; learning from members about how to fulfill needs and connecting to resources; empowering members and interns alike; persistence in getting funds; tailored advice and support (especially RCDI); constant debriefing; cultivating and stewarding relationships.
Systemic	Adapting to needs in different regions of the district—RCDI, Telecomm; building on history of cooperatives; allowing governing council to make final decisions (organizational cultutre); utilizing mentors; giving interns time to adapt (organizational culture); time to joke. Increased collaboration among members; learning about members' needs and connecting at meetings; learning funder criteria; influencing the reassignment of CTED staff; all collaborations, especially with NETCSC

Table 4. Leadership dimensions and examples in the Columbia-Pacific RC&EDD case

Discussion

Action Learning occurs in complex environments, characterized by continual learning and re-learning, credibility and emergence

(Garratt, 1983; Pedlar, Burgoyne & Brook, 2005; Revans, 1982), critical perspectives that catalyze change (Garratt, 1983; Revans, 1982), connectedness and community (Revans, 1982) and creativity and sensemaking (Garratt, 1983; Revans, 1982). We can look to Complexity Leadership Theory (Hazy & Uhl-Bien, 2002; Lichtenstein, et al., 2006; Marion & Uhl-Bien, 2002; and McKelvey, 2001) to learn how leadership of organizations appears in complex adaptive systems. Nonprofit organizations tend to be complex because they operate primarily in the relationship end of the task-relationship continuum (Northouse, 2009).

Two nonprofit organizations were studied to (1) determine whether Action Learning characteristics were observed, (2) how leadership was displayed in this environment, and (3) how these two sets of characteristics connect. These two organizations could be considered to be successful in their adoption of complexity; Habitat for Humanity of Grays Harbor was created in a community not previously serving the need of decent affordable housing and Columbia-Pacific RC&EDD transformed from a single-issue organization to expanding service to more comprehensively serve its communities.

Participants in both HFHOGH and Columbia-Pacific RC&EDD knew their community well and were willing to learn from each other, representing credibility in Complexity Leadership Theory. They exploited complexity by inviting participation from others while willingly sharing expertise and time. They emphasized trust and open communication, understanding their role in the community, ongoing evaluation, and taking a systemic perspective while building their organizations incrementally. This required a commitment from all participants.

It was the adaptability of the organizations that permitted them to move through the changes in a rapidly changing environment. Members strategically communicated with each other frequently between regular meetings, a function that was necessary for boards of directors that both governed and were "working boards." The organizations turned negative aspects of the community into assets. For example, abandoned properties and the inability of banks to sell foreclosed properties meant that HFHOGH did not have to pay for land to build its first six homes demonstrating creativity. An entrepreneurial attitude throughout the leadership meant that visibility was high and made positive with each new success. Support for initiatives came from parties not ordinarily expected to participate, such as local governments, local banks, and two locally-important foundations for HFHOCH and coalitions outside the District for Columbia-Pacific RC&EDD. These non-traditional supporters were pursued only after open discussion by all participants.

Habitat for Humanity affiliates have a fairly straightforward purpose — to partner with qualifying low-income families in a community to pursue home ownership. Affiliates, including the one in this case, adapted standardized policies in the pursuit of their purpose. Still, low-income housing development is a complex undertaking involving multiple legal issues, land use, community development, preparing partner families for homeownership, recruiting community and volunteer support, and the construction of safe, reliable homes.

The study of Columbia-Pacific RC&EDD's immersion into complexity corresponds with the findings of Marion & Uhl-Bien (2002) and others, identifying characteristics of leadership in complex adaptive systems during the organization's transformation. The future desired states emerged from ongoing interactions between agents, both internally and externally. Leadership modeled learning and adaptation via interactions among diverse and affected participants.

Leadership enables, via interactions among participants, rather than directs change in complex systems (Plowman et al., 2007). Dispersed leadership in such a complex environment makes sense. No one person is likely to hold sufficient expertise to lead through the multiple scenarios found in complexity, instead leading collectively and participatively. Indeed, rather than wrest control, nominal leaders encouraged others to lead when necessary and saw their role as coordinator (and sometimes spokesperson). Although one person's name was designated to represent the organization on correspondence to outside entities, that correspondence was usually drafted by experts or those with connections to collaborating organizations. Participants and sub-committees were relied upon to review proposed policies and recommend any adaptations, then relied upon to determine how to implement their policies while reporting fully to each other and soliciting feedback.

The nominal leaders at both organizations did play a key role in the exploitation of complexity that occurred, not by using legitimate power to specify or direct change but by creating conditions that allowed for the emergence of such change, including efforts to maintain distributed leadership and referent power. Participants became comfortable with complexity — overlap, interdependence, adaptiveness and co-evolution — a state from which novelty could emerge. At the same time, participants also provided some order (sensemaking) by interpreting and giving meaning to the actions of collective, successive innovation as progress was made and encouraged each other and their organizations to be innovative.

In complex systems, leadership enables, via interactions among participants, rather than directs change in complex systems. Dispersed leadership in such a complex environment makes sense. No one person is likely to hold sufficient expertise to lead through the multiple scenarios and intersectionality found in complexity. Indeed, rather than take control nominal leaders encouraged others to lead when necessary and saw their role as coordinator (and sometimes spokesperson).

The findings suggest that Action Learning leadership played an important role in giving meaning to what was happening, changing what it is that people talked about in the organization. As the radical shift in identity began to emerge at Columbia-Pacific RC&EDD, participants spent less time talking about how to turn around a stagnant organization and more time talking about the best ways to serve their constituents and communities. HFHOGH began strategizing beyond home building for needy families to eliminate all substandard housing in its service area. Finally, it was found that by using an appreciative approach, managing words rather than people is important in encouraging change. The language that is adopted helps people understand what is happening in the organization.

A most unique feature of the organizations studied in this case was that leadership was shared among participants—stewardship was collective. The impulse towards instability counter-balanced the impulse towards stability through differences in style found in individuals who shared leadership, keeping the system from swirling into complete chaos.

Limitations, Delimitations, and Suggestions for Further Research

Although case studies offer fine-grained detail of organizational phenomenon, one concern should always be the generalizability of the findings. This research relied on a sample size of two in a qualitative study as the foundation for the theoretical propositions offered. In addition, both are nonprofit organizations. However, nonprofit organizations operating in different environments, nonprofit organizations are increasingly recognizing the complex environments in which they operate. Propositions in this case can likely be replicated in future research as more organizations identify characteristics of Complexity Leadership Theory.

This study did not investigate any correlation between sources or practices of power and the leadership characteristics. During the five-year period of this study, power appeared relatively balanced, with slight variations due to differences in practices of expert power, reward power based in resources available, and perhaps some legitimate power. Communication was heterarchical and quite transparent and collegial, with the good of the constituents in the overall populations for each organization's service areas continually emphasized by inviting multiple and diverse participants. However, there was no assurance this balance or collegiality could be maintained as participants entered and departed the organization. Trust seemed to be a key element in dispersed leadership and in the processes and procedures. That was a variable that was not addressed by this study; if trust among the participants changes, is high functionality within a complex environment, as observed in these cases, sustainable?

In the study, emergent self-organizing behavior led to a successful transformation of the organization and behaviors were observed that seemed to enable this successful self organizing. An important area of study could be whether there are differences in the way leaders enable emergence that contribute to failures rather than successes. If any one of the leadership characteristics is absent, will the system be pushed too far into chaos or stagnancy? For example, if insufficient attention is given to non-linear interactions, or providing meaning to the changes that are happening is not accomplished, will emergent innovation fail? On the other hand, can all the leadership characteristics be present and an unsuccessful exploitation of complexity still occur? Future research can explore attention to unsuccessful as well as successful transformations in complex environments and the associated leadership practices.

This study was undertaken by wondering what the role of leadership is in organizations embedded in and exploiting complex adaptive environments using Action Learning. These two cases demonstrate that effective leadership in Action Learning environments is different from traditional perspectives, in that it is more distributed and not resting in one particular "heroic" individual. Participants who step into and out of leadership roles during Action Learning processes are effective in catalyzing change to help organizations make the best of the moment, commonly without knowing what is going to happen next.

Conflict of interest statement

I have no conflicts of interest to disclose. There are no sponsors or any other funders for this project. I am the sole author of this original manuscript.

References

Alaimo, S. P. (2008) Nonprofits and evaluation: Managing expectations from the leader's perspective. In: Carman, J. G. & Fredericks, K. A. (eds.), *Nonprofits and evaluation. New directions for evaluation.* San Francisco, Wiley, pp. 73-92.

Alexander, V. D. (1998) Environmental constraints and organizational strategies: Complexity, conflict, and coping in the nonprofit sector. In: Powell, W. W. & Clemens, E. S. (eds.), *Private Action and the Public Good.* New Haven, CT, Yale University Press, pp. 272-290.

Anderson, R. (1999) Complexity theory and organization science. *Organization Science.* 10 (3), 216–232.

Ashmos, D. P., Duchon, D., McDaniel, R. R., & Huonker, J. W. (2002) What a mess! Participation as a simple managerial rule to 'complexify' organizations. *Journal of Management Studies.* 39 (2), 189–206.

Boisot, M. & Child, J. (1999) Organizations as adaptive systems in complex environments: The case of China, *Organization Science: A Journal of the Institute of Management Sciences.* 10 (3), 237-252.

Capra, F. (1996) *The web of life.* New York, Anchor Books Doubleday.

Chiles, T., Meyer, A. & Hench, T. (2004) Organizational emergence: The origin and transformation of Branson, Missouri's musical theaters. *Organization Science.* 15 (5), 499–519.

Collins, J. (2001) Level 5 leadership: The triumph of humility and fierce resolve. *Harvard Business Review.* 79 (1), 66–76.

Dozois, E., Langlois, M., & Blancet-Cohen, B. (2010) *A practitioner's guide to developmental evaluation.* Montreal, J. W. McConnell Foundation.

Eisenhardt, K. M. (1989) Making fast strategic decisions in high-velocity environments. *Academy of Management Journal.* 32 (3), 543–576.

Foster, J. (2005) From simplistic to complex systems in economics. *Cambridge Journal of Economics.* 29 (6), 873-892.

Gamble, J. A. (2008) *A developmental evaluation primer.* Montreal, J. W. McConnell Family Foundation.

Garratt, B. (1983) The power of action learning. In: Pedlar, M. (ed.) *Action learning in practice.* 4th ed. Oxfordshire, England, Routledge, pp. 21-34.

Hazy, J. K. & Uhl-Bien, M. (2012) Changing the rules: The implications of complexity science for leadership research and practice. In: Day, D. (ed.) *The Oxford handbook of leadership and organizations.* Oxford, Oxford University Press, pp. 709-732.

Holland, J. H. (1995) *Hidden order.* Reading, MA, Addison-Wesley Publishing.

Isabella, L. A. (1990) Evolving interpretations as a change unfolds: How managers construe key organizational events. *Academy of Management Journal.* 33 (1), 7-41.

Kauffman, S. (1993) *The origins of order: Self-organization and selection in evolution.* New York, Oxford University Press.

Kember, D. (2000) *Action learning and action research: Improving the quality of teaching and learning.* London, Psychology Press.

Kerr, S. & Jermier, J. M. (1978) Substitutes for leadership: Their meaning and measurement, *Organizational Behavior & Human Performance.* 22 (3), 375-403.

Kotter, J. P. (1985) *Power and influence: Beyond formal authority.* New York, Free Press.

Kotter, J. P. (1990) *A force for change: How leadership differs from management.* New York, Free Press.

Kotter, J. P. (1996) *Leading change.* Boston: Harvard Business School Press.

Langley, A. (1999) Strategies for theorizing from process data. *Academy of Management Review.* 24, 691-710.

Lichtenstein, B. B., Uhl-Bien, M., Marion, R., Seers, A., Orton, J. D. & Schreiber, C. (2006) Complexity leadership theory: An interactive perspective on leading in complex adaptive systems. *Emergence: Complexity and Organization.* 8 (4), 2-12.

Lizzio, A. & Wilson, K. (2004) Action learning in higher education: An investigation of its potential to develop professional capability. *Studies in Higher Education.* 29 (4), 469-488.

Luhmann, N. (1995) *Social systems.* Stanford, Stanford University Press.

Maguire, S. & McKelvey, B. (1999) Complexity and management: Moving from fad to firm foundations. *Emergence.* 1 (2), 19-61.

Marion, R., & Uhl-Bien, M. (2002) Leadership in complex organizations. *The Leadership Quarterly.* 12(4), 389-418.

McGill, I. & Beaty, L. (2001) *Action learning: a guide for professional, management & educational development.* London, Psychology Press.

McKelvey, B. (1999) Avoiding complexity catastrophe in coevolutionary pockets: Strategies for rugged landscapes. *Organization Science.* 10 (3), 294-321.

McKelvey, B. (2001) What is complexity science? It is really order-creation science. *Emergence.* 3 (1), 137–157.

McKelvey, B., & Lichtenstein, B. (2007) Leadership in the four stages of emergence. *Complex Systems Leadership Theory.* 1, 93–108.

Merriam, S. B. & Tisdell, E .J. (2016) *Qualitative research: A guide to design and implementation.* San Francisco, John Wiley and Sons.

Miles, M. B. & Huberman, A. M. (1994) *Qualitative data analysis.* Thousand Oaks, CA, Sage.

Mitchell, M. (2009) *Complexity: A guided tour.* New York, Oxford University Press.

Northouse, P. (2009) Introduction to leadership: Concepts and practice. Thousand Oaks, CA, SAGE.

Patton MQ (2016) *Developmental evaluation exemplars: Principles in practice.* New York, Guilford Press.

Pedler, M., Burgoyne, J. & Brook, C. (2005) What has action learning learned to become? *Action Learning: Research and Practice.* 2 (1), 49-68.

Plowman, D. A., Solansky, S. T., Beck, T. E., Baker, L, Kulkarni, M, & Travis, D.V. (2007) The role of leadership in emergent, self-organization. *The Leadership Quarterly.* 18, 341–35.

Prigogine, I. (1997) *The end of uncertainty: Time, chaos, and new laws of nature.* New York, Free Press.

Regine, B. & Lewin, R. (2000) Leading at the edge: How leaders influence complex systems. *Emergence.* 2 (2), 5–23.

Revans, R.W. (1982) What is action learning? *Journal of Management Development.* 1 (3). 64-75.

Schein, E. H. (2017) *Organizational culture and leadership.* 5th ed. Hoboken, NJ, John Wiley & Sons.

Schwartz, P. (1991) *The art of the long view: Planning for the future in an uncertain world.* New York, Doubleday.

Stacey, R. (1992) *Managing the unknowable.* San Francisco, Jossey–Bass Publishers.

Stacey, R. (1995) The science of complexity: An alternative perspective for strategic change processes. *Strategic Management Journal.* 16, 477–495.

Uhl-Bien, M., Marion, R. & McKelvey, B. (2007) Complexity leadership theory: Shifting leadership from the industrial age to the knowledge era. *The Leadership Quarterly.* 18 (4), 298-318.

Wheatley, M. (1999) *Leadership and the new science.* San Francisco, Berrett-Koehler.

Yin, R. K. (2003) *Case study research. 3rd ed.* Thousand Oaks, Sage Publication.

Zuber-Skerritt, O. (1993) Improving learning and teaching through action learning and action research. *Higher Education Research and Development.* 12 (1), 45-58.

Biography

Terrence Fernsler, MNPL, PhD, has been a nonprofit professional for over 40 years. After earning his Ph.D. in Strategic Leadership (Nonprofit and Community Leadership concentration) at James Madison University in the United States, he has been teaching undergraduate and graduate students in Nonprofit Studies. His primary research interests are an extension of his nonprofit practice, helping others apply complexity theory to public service leadership, including his current interest in applying action learning. Dr. Fernsler seeks to catalyze bridging theory and practice by presenting findings of research in sustainable leadership in complex environments — including presentations at nine conferences in the last seven years.

Engendering customer care and complaints handling in Government real estate companies in the Caribbean: change from below through action research

Erica Prentice and Ali Rostron

Abstract

This paper examines why attempts to improve customer care and customer relationship management in a Caribbean Government real estate company continued to fail. The lead author undertook an action research study as an insider researcher. One macro action research cycle was completed using multiple data sources and with key customer facing employees as an action research group to engage in collaborative inquiry. The results showed that the transactional nature of the landlord-tenant relationship, the fetter of being a State Enterprise, executive inertia, and silo thinking and behaviour made implementing change an intractable problem. However, the study also reveals the potential for "bottom-up" change through collaboration and capacity building with staff. We contribute both to knowledge of customer care in the public sector and to management practice, by showing how change can be achieved without top management support.

Key words: Action research, Customer Relationship Management, Special Purpose State Enterprise, Caribbean, landlord and tenant

What is known about the topic?

There is little research on customer care and customer complaints handling in Special Purpose State Enterprises (SPSEs), especially those that are Caribbean landlords. There have been many complaints about customer care delivery in the Public Sector and despite movement towards embracing Customer Relationship Management (CRM), Caribbean landlords who manage SPSEs continue to lag due to their limited focus on customer centricity.

What does this paper add?

The paper adds to the limited research on customer care delivery in a land-based SPSE in the Caribbean. It reveals the challenges facing Public Sector organisations and specifically Public Sector landlords, but it also demonstrates how the concerted effort of a dedicated cross- functional team can engender change from bottom up through participative action research

Who will benefit from its content?

Public Sector Real Estate Practitioners, Managers in SPSEs in the Caribbean and all who manage property on behalf of the Government

What is the relevance to AL and AR scholars and practitioners?

The research demonstrates how managers can conduct insider action researcher with co-workers as research partners to solve organisational problems. Practitioners who work on organisational problems demonstrate the potential of the AR process to assist them in enhancing their practice as agents in engendering organisational change supported by their staff

Received   October 2023   Reviewed November 2023   Published December 2024

Introduction

Notwithstanding reforms in the public sector in Small Island Developing States (SIDS) in the Caribbean, the overall level of customer satisfaction with public sector delivery of goods and services remains low, and the call for a strategy to deliver better service to customers throughout Government Departments is ongoing (Smith and Charles 2018). This reflects a wider concern in which private sector companies appear to be more successful in embracing and applying Customer Relationship Management (CRM) principles to enhance organisational performance than public sector entities (Kumar and Reinartz 2018). This includes the real estate sector. For the public sector, and especially government landlords in SIDS, the issue is all the more pressing as island governments reduce subventions to these agencies. These agencies are mandated to be more commercially viable and therefore in need of maintaining customer satisfaction, but the focus on financial viability may also be to the detriment of attention paid to customer care.

This paper presents an account of an action research project undertaken by the lead author, at 'Real Estate Solutions Limited' (RESL)[1] which aimed to address the persistent high numbers of customer complaints and low levels of customer satisfaction. RESL is a Special Purpose State Enterprise (SPSE) which reports to a Government Ministry in one of the SIDS in the Caribbean. The company has a portfolio of industrial properties comprising 772.13 hectares of land and is landlord to more than 300 tenants who are involved in light manufacturing. Some of the tenants lease land, while others lease factories owned by RESL. Since 2013, RESL has been mandated by the Government to become commercially viable, due to reducing subventions and dwindling returns from oil and natural gas, the mainstay of the country's economy. As a landlord, RESL has focused on asset management and facilitated the development of economic zones. In RESL's Strategic Plan for 2018 to 2022 (p. 12), its stated mission is: 'A catalyst for growth of businesses in the non-oil and gas sector by providing real estate solutions, which leverage the talents and passion of our people.' It further envisions itself as 'Providing innovative and sustainable real estate solutions that deliver lasting value to tenants, shareholders and society.' (Strategic Plan for 2018 to 2022, p. 12).

In this regard, RESL can be seen reflecting wider Western trends within the public sector and the implementation of New Public Management paradigms.

In 2015, a tenant satisfaction survey found that only 55% of tenants expressed general satisfaction with the company as their landlord. One of the ongoing complaints from tenants was the lengthy time that RESL took to effect repairs to their buildings so that they could

---

[1] 'Real Estate Solutions Limited' is a pseudonym for the company to protect it and its employees.

resume normal business operations. The delays commonly resulted in tenants withholding rent. As a result of not treating repairs and complaints expeditiously, the company experienced significant loss of revenue, as well as increasing aged receivables, non-renewal of leases, and voids.

In 2015, a Customer Care Management Project was initiated with the aim of implementing a Customer Care Management Plan targeting the company's tenants in order to improve the landlord-tenant relationship and customer care delivery. The stated deliverables included a Customer Care Management Action Plan and a customer-centred service delivery process. In 2017, the company began an exercise to prepare a new Strategic Plan for 2018-22. There was an acknowledgment that a key weakness was that the organisation lacked an understanding of the needs of its customers, and one of the company's new strategic themes was Customer Service Excellence. Despite this, and subsequent re-launches, the original Customer Care Management Project was not sustained, and failed to achieve its intended outcomes.

The lead author was formerly a Manager in the Real Estate Assets Department (READ) for thirteen years. Her role included overseeing all lease administration transactions related to tenants. As a Manager, she felt responsible for addressing the longstanding organisational problem of the need for system improvement in real estate administration, and also wanted to improve practice for herself and her team as they dispensed real estate services to tenants. Specifically, she wanted to make a significant change in how customer care was delivered within RESL, and more importantly, secure its strategic significance to the organisation. The lead author was also a Doctor of Business Administration (DBA) candidate who decided to focus her thesis on why attempts at customer centric initiatives at RESL continued to fail.

The research project aimed to answer the following questions:

1. Why have attempts to improve customer care and customer relationship management at RESL continued to fail?

2. What actions are required to embed customer care policies and practices within RESL?

Literature review

Corporate Real Estate Management and customer care

Corporate Real Estate Management (CREM) as a discipline recognises a company's real estate portfolio as a tangible asset. It therefore plays a strategic role in the life of the organisation through the provision of land and built accommodation (van den Beemt-Tjeerdsma and Veuger, 2016) to ensure a significant return on investment (Buttle and Maklan, 2019). Heywood (2011) and Sulaiman et al. (2015) have noted that the real estate portfolio of many organisations is not strategically managed in a manner that supports the business processes of the organisation. Similarly, many organisations are devoid of systems which enable them to effectively execute the activity of CREM (Haynes and Haynes, 2012; Lalloo, 2013). In the public sector context, Marona (2016) lauds the introduction of New Public Management (NPM) as an opportunity for public sector Real Estate Managers to address managerial deficiencies and also to enhance real estate management processes, particularly in order to provide better value for money for tax payers and to reduce financial burdens on governments (Kask, 2014).

Given the role of CREM for the economic viability of the organisation, the relationship between landlord and tenant is a vital one (Edwards and Ellison, 2004). It has therefore been argued that tenants should be seen as customers (Palm, 2011) and this relationship understood as a form of Customer Relationship Management (CRM) in which the organisation builds a long-lasting relationship with the customer and delivers value to the customer based on customers' needs and expectations (Kumar and Reinartz, 2018). As and when such expectations are not met, customers may raise complaints. Complaints can therefore be a rich source of concrete information for businesses (Hsiao et al., 2016) to enable them to ultimately strengthen relationships with customers, providing that the organisation has effective systems to capture and satisfactorily address complaints, and for information from complaints to inform the strategic decision-making process of the organisation (Stauss and Seidel, 2019).

Nevertheless, the implementation of CRM systems remains challenging (Bibiano, Marco-Simó and Pastor, 2014) with up to 70% of CRM projects failing due to poor implementation (Farhan Abed & Ellatif, 2018). It requires a holistic approach combining people, processes and technology to create a customer-centric organisation (Rababah, Mohd & Ibrahim, 2011). One of the most important factors for successful CRM implementation is the support of and commitment from top management (Bibiano et al., 2014; Farhan et al., 2018; Kumar, 2012; Mohd, Rababah & Ibrahim., 2011; Tekin, 2013) through the integration of business functions to better deliver customer value. The adoption of cross-functional processes as opposed to silo behaviour and mentality is also highlighted by Kumar (2012), while Farhan et al. (2018) further emphasise the importance of all staff involvement and an organisation culture which is customer focused to facilitate meeting the needs of customers.

The public sector context

Corporate Real Estate Management in the public sector brings particular challenges. Public entities may regard property assets that they manage as a public good rather than as a productive asset (Hanis, Trigunarsyah and Susilawati, 2011; Kaganova and Nayyar-Stone, 2000) and are commonly viewed as needing to move from a reactionary to a strategic approach to property management (Boakye-Agyeman and Bugri, 2019; Gibson, 2006; Wojewnik-Filipkowska, Rymarzak, and Lausberg, 2015). In line with this, it is argued that public sector landlords need to re-frame how they define and treat occupants of their properties, not just as tenants and sources of cash-flow, but as customers whose loyalty and behaviours can be enhanced through good customer service and customer care (Kivlehan, 2011).

Despite the New Public Management drive towards a more commercial approach, the public sector continues to also be expected to sustain a commitment to social responsibilities and public value. Public real estate management therefore has been characterised as 'quasi-public' or 'social businesses' (Collier, 2005; Gruis & Nieboer, 2004). For example, occupiers of public sector properties do not always pay the full market price for leasing arrangements, and there may be an expectation that the Government will support their businesses in difficult economic times while overlooking breaches of their leasehold covenants. Conversely, public sector landlords may continue to be dependent on Central Government for funding to effect maintenance related repairs for tenants in occupation of built accommodation, with such dependency further exacerbated by five-year political cycles.

There is also a debate regarding the applicability of framing tenants as customers within a public service context. Fountain (2001) points out that the mere use of the word "customer" is sorely inadequate and the borrowing of terminology from the private sector will not work because it also relies on underpinning private sector paradigms and strategies. Public sector organisations continue to provide services of public value to citizens, rather than customers who actively choose services (Buttle & Maklan, 2019; Thomas, 2013). Particularly when it comes to leasing of real estate, it is not a simple undertaking for a business to pack up and leave, and there are many logistical, employee related and locational issues which propel businesses to decide on a specific location in the first place. Equally, the type of customers that public sector landlords attract may not be able to afford to lease in the private real estate market and as such are compelled to rent at social market rates.

There has been little research to date on Customer Relationship Management in the public sector, and still less in public sector CREM in developing countries such as the Caribbean islands. Nevertheless, what little evidence there is (Pareja et al., 2016; Smith and Charles, 2018) suggests that levels of satisfaction with public sector services continue to be low, transactional in nature and characterised by lengthy processing times. The organisation discussed in this paper therefore reflects a wider issue with which public organisations including public landlords continue to wrestle.

Methodology

As a manager seeking to not only understand, but to improve customer care in RESL, the lead author chose action research as the most suitable method for her investigation. Action research generates knowledge which is actionable and can prove useful to the insider action researcher and the organisation under study (Coghlan and Brannick, 2010; Saunders, Lewis and Thornhill, 2016). Planning and taking action are integral to the method of action research and the result of the action can change the strategic direction of the organisation under inquiry. **Figure 1** is relevant. The collaborative nature of action research requires the research participants to function effectively as a team as opposed to a group of disparate individuals (Abraham, 2012; Johnson and Duberley, 2012). For Creswell (2013), it is enquiry completed with others where the voice of the participants is heard throughout the process. In engaging in action research, the lead author was able to

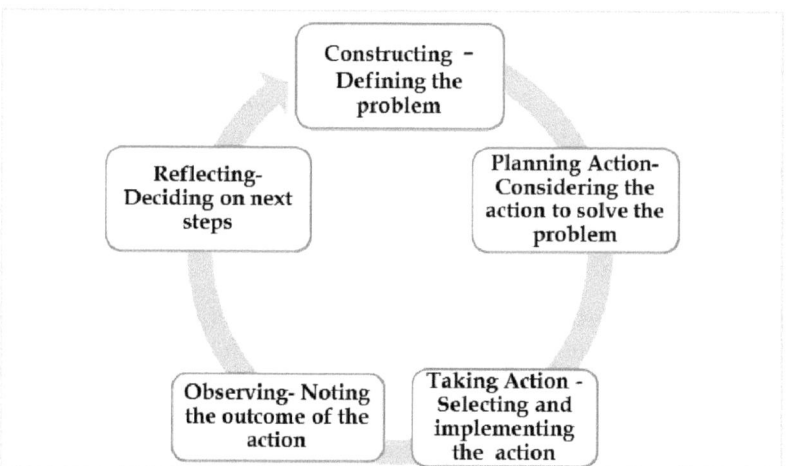

Figure 1: Action Research Cycle
Source: Adapted from Coghlan and Brannick (2010)

involve staff from the Real Estate Department as both subjects and co-researchers in order to effect change in the company, with decisions being made collaboratively at every step of the inquiry.

Due to both the time constraints of the DBA programme and because RESL only allowed limited time during working hours to convene action research group meetings, it was only possible to undertake one macro level action research cycle of diagnosing, planning action, taking action and evaluating actions taken.

Gaining Access: Ethical Issues and Considerations of the Inquiry

As an employee of RESL for over 13 years, primary access for the lead author was not problematic. She received consent from the President of the company on 16 September 2016 to begin the intervention. One of the issues which arose was the process for data collection and establishment of the action research group. Initially, the lead author was advised that all group meetings should take place during lunch periods, but she was subsequently able to obtain approval from her own manager to conduct some of the meetings during working hours as she was also the team lead for Customer Care and Management.

As an insider action researcher, the lead author was conscious of the subversiveness of her action (Coghlan and Brannick, 2010) in operating in the dual role as overt and covert researcher. While the action research group was aware of her DBA and the research project, her reflections, actions and journaling of experiences remained covert.

The potential murkiness of role duality was mitigated by ongoing rigorous self-questioning and reflection on her position as employee and action researcher. In particular, reflections on her practice with the action research group and the interpersonal nature of the inquiry into customer care delivery at RESL led to increasing dialogue with all participants as the action research phases developed. The lead author's reflections helped her to recognise that participants brought valuable experiences to the inquiry and knowledge of the operations of the company using different lenses. Essentially, they were co-creating knowledge to better serve the company and create value.

Formation of the Action Research Group

In July 2018, the lead author requested Departmental Vice Presidents to identify potentially suitable employees to participate in the action research group (ARG). Representation from many Departments was needed in order to investigate and take action on customer care as an organisational issue requiring the involvement and co-operation of all business units, not just those directly dealing with tenants and properties. Once the selected employees agreed to be a part of the action research group, they were required to complete a consent form and were advised that they were free to discontinue if they so desired. All the participants remained and contributed to the process until the end. The final group of ten staff included members from Property Management, Maintenance, Finance, Human Resources, Corporate Communications and Administration with a range of years of service from six months to twelve years.

Data Generation

Data were generated from a range of sources at each stage of the action research cycle. **Figure 2** illustrates the key data sources mapped against each stage of the macro level action research cycle.

In the Diagnosing Phase, the lead author sought to understand and construct the precise nature of the problem of customer care, and to integrate findings with the extant literature. In order to examine corporate attitudes, perceptions, language and policies in relation to customer care and the organisation's tenants, and their relationship with the organisation, the lead author reviewed the two most recent corporate strategic plans (2013-2015 and 2018-2022), and conducted semi-structured interviews with three senior managers across estate management, property management and human resource management. To investigate the experiences and perceptions of tenants, the recent tenant satisfaction survey was reviewed, and the organisation's tenant records analysed in order to build up a typical case example of how tenant complaints were handled.

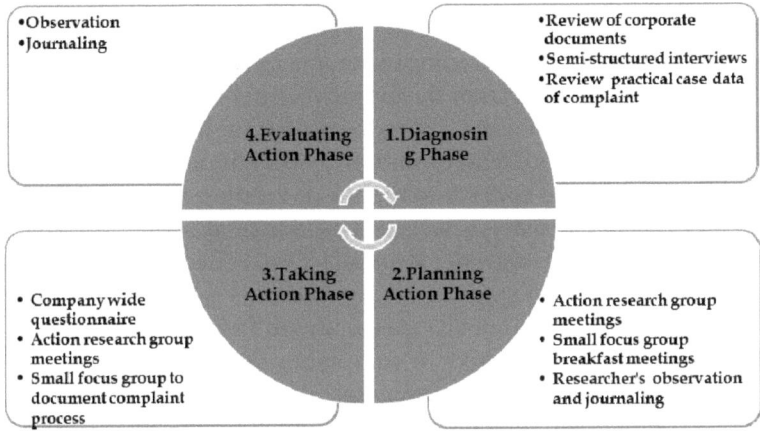

Figure 2: Data Sources Mapped Against Phases of Macro Action Research Cycle

In the Planning Action stage, the lead author collected data from both formal organisational breakfast meetings in her capacity as leader of the strategic initiative for Customer Care and Management, and Action Research Group meetings in the form of observational notes and reflective journaling. At all action research group meetings, minutes were taken by a group member for confirmation at the following meeting. Data were similarly collected as the ARG started to take action (plus a further diagnostic survey of staff) and as action was then evaluated.

Data were also generated throughout from the lead author's direct involvement in the lease administration process at RESL, including interactions with the tenants, receiving complaints and collaboration with members of the different Departments.

Data Analysis

Content analysis was used to analyse corporate strategic documents (stage 1, Diagnosis). This analysis focused primarily on the language used to describe the tenants of RESL, and the context in which different language or terms were used. The analysis was also focused on any change or development in language or ideology between the two Strategic Plans in relation to customer care and complaints management. Thematic analysis was used to analyse interviews with senior managers (stage 1, Diagnosis) and qualitative comments from the employee survey (stage 3, Taking Action). This followed the common process for thematic analysis (King and Horrocks, 2010) of initially coding transcribed text and aggregating related codes into higher-order themes and sub-themes. Thematic analysis was also used to analyse the meeting notes of the ARG, researcher journaling and reflections (stage 2, Planning Action and stage 3, Taking Action). Customer complaint handling (stage 1, Diagnosis) was analysed through case analysis, by selecting a small number of complaints and tracking their progress from initial customer contact through to final resolution, and mapping the interactions with different organisational Departments.

Applying Action Research: Diagnosing the problem

In the following section, as lead author and insider action researcher, I present a first-person account of the outcomes of the AR cycle from the perspective of someone intimately involved with RESL and the problems that were under investigation.

Corporate Strategic Plans

Analysis of the corporate strategic documents revealed that RESL used the words "tenant" and "customer" variously depending on the context, giving the impression that tenants and customers were viewed as separate entities rather than one and the same individual.

Overall, reference to "tenant" outweighed references to "customer" by two to one (68 references to tenant and 31 to customer). "Customer" was typically used as part of explicit reference to service delivery, customer care and a customer-focused approach; in other words, where the term "customer" is at the heart of the process being discussed. However, both Strategic Plans more commonly referred to tenants as part of addressing the organisation's relationship with them as a landlord, in association with "lease", "marketable title", remittance of rent and occupation.

The findings thus support the observation by Kivlehan (2011, p. 3) that to consider 'occupiers as customers requires a shift in perception about the relationship between Landlords and tenants'. Based on the pattern and context of usage of the word "tenant" and "customer" coupled with the more frequent use of the word "tenant", evidently the concept of "tenant" as opposed to "customer" was more significant in the corporate life of RESL and used in a very legalistic context without apparent awareness of the switch in language.

Tables 1 and 2 present the keywords-in-context which demonstrate the two narratives used by RESL and the context in which the two words were used in each Strategic Plan.

Context for Use of Tenant	Context for Use of Customer
Real estate assets performance	New applicant
Clear and marketable title	New site development
Remittance of rent	Service delivery
Transactions with the company	Discussion around management of real estate assets
Reference to a lease, re-entry of property or legal relationship	Enhancement of service delivery
Onboarding of a new entity	

Table 1: Analysis of keywords-in- Context: Two Narratives from the 2013 to 2015 Strategic Plan

Context for use of Tenant	Context for use of Customer
Delivering value	Collaboration
Populating new sites	Innovative solutions
Optimising existing sites	Service oriented culture
Improving networks and partnerships	
Legal title	
Remittance of rent	
Regaining possession of property	
Beneficial occupation	

Table 2: Analysis of keywords-in-context: Two Narratives from the 2018 to 2022 Strategic Plan

Comparing the language of the 2013 Plan to that of the 2018 Plan, very little had changed in the way the company viewed its occupiers as the context for word usage remained the same.

Senior manager interviews

The interviews with the three members of the executive team of RESL generated five overarching themes incorporating 21 codes (**table 3 refers**).

Codes	Themes
Focus on lease covenants It is a landlord- tenant relationship Partner not tenant Unstructured to deliver customer care No landlord-tenant synergy	Purely Transactional Relationship
Reengineer complaints process Gaps in handling queries No structured approach for complaints Complaints not logged, no standards	Just a Complaint
Adherence to policies No flexibility to act Constrained by guidelines Can't raise own capital Spread thinly	Fetter of being a SPSE
No seamless process between Departments No alignment of systems	Guarding Territory
No subvention Funding issue Bare bones Project failure due to funding No follow through by executives	Failures due to lack of funding and executive inaction

Table 3: Interview Codes and Themes

A consistent message from all three executives was that RESL operated within a very rigid organisational structure governed by strict rules of engagement as determined by the Government. In this regard, it can be said that RESL as a SPSE reflected a Western style of management practice given the influential role of Government decision making into the affairs of the company supported by its Board of Directors. As a public body subject to five-year political cycles, its programmes and projects are dictated primarily by the political directorate rather than to benefit its tenants. The five themes that were identified have revealed different dimensions of this espoused reality.

The first theme is the fetter of being a State Enterprise. Executives expressed regret that the organisation could not do more for tenants: "if we were privately managed, we could do much more, however we are constrained by guidelines and there is no subvention." In particular, the need to "adhere to policies" means that there is no flexibility to be able to offer tenants what they want.

The fetter of being a State Enterprise also meant that the vagaries of changing politicians every five years resulted in changes to executive management and Board Directors, meaning that strategic projects were typically started, but not seen through to completion.

A second, related theme is funding constraints. Executives observed that budgetary cuts to State Enterprises were not easily replaced despite the mandate to become commercially viable. The reduced funding led to "little preventative maintenance" and was also blamed for the failure of many strategic projects including attempts to centre and improve customer care. "We are relying on bare bones; we are State and spread thinly. Initiatives such as CRM failed due to funding and the focus of the organisation shifted."

The executives were more divided on their view of the organisation's relationship with tenants. The most senior executive argued strongly for a purely formal and transactional relationship, and emphasised its legal nature and reciprocal rights and responsibilities: "We manage just the lease; it is a landlord-tenant relationship. The tenant must honour the covenants." The same executive further suggested that any ambiguity in the relationship should be avoided in order to ensure tenant compliance and income from the lease: "The organisation's focus should be on the leasehold covenants in order to erase any ambiguity in the mind of the tenant." However, the other two executives acknowledged this reality whilst also suggesting a different perspective:

> To be honest, based on previous experience how we deal with tenants, we do not treat them as a serious stakeholder, that's my personal view. We should see them as a customer and a very important customer, and I can be wrong.

A fourth theme to emerge was that RESL does not have an effective or consistent complaints handling process, beyond receiving them from tenants. A complaint remains "just a complaint." Executives confirmed that there is no standard process for logging or tracking complaints, that outcomes depend primarily on whether funds are available to remedy repairs and that "there are no established customer care standards."

The final theme was 'Guarding Territory'. Executives commented that Departments worked within strict spheres of responsibility and there was little communication between them, which has implications for customer complaint handling. For example, one executive confirmed that on completion of any repair works following a tenant complaint, feedback would only go to Finance and not the requesting Department or the Assets and Lease Administration Departments.

Complaints process analysis

The final stage of diagnosis was to analyse how complaints were handled by RESL. No records of complaint management and resolution were kept, and so as the lead author, I tracked the progress of all complaints received during a three-month period. During a three-month period, I documented 25 complaints. As the majority were maintenance-related they were treated as maintenance requests and sent to the Maintenance Department, with no systematic consideration of underlying issues or possible preventative measures that could be implemented. Limited funding and the need for compliance with Government procurement regulations meant that there was a long and protracted system in place to engage contractors to effect repairs to buildings. There was no system of updating or target deadlines, and updates appeared to be only instigated by further tenant complaints and emails from one Department to another, with long periods of apparent inaction in-between.

The tenant satisfaction survey revealed that, in addition to overall low levels of satisfaction with RESL (55%) and complaint handling (52%), tenants were particularly dissatisfied with the time taken to effect any issues raised, especially repairs:

> Problems are very slowly dealt with and tenants are losing their money and business; Complaint issues should be resolved within a reasonable timeframe-months not years, not swept under the carpet.

Several tenants suggested that the problem lay not with the officers they dealt with directly, but that "they are limited in making decisions" and "need support internally." Tenants also highlighted the contrast between dealing with RESL and a private enterprise: "Were we dealing with a commercial, private sector landlord, we would have been able to sit down, understand each other's viewpoints and come to a quick and hopefully fair settlement."

Applying Action Research: Planning action

As the lead author, my diagnosis of the problem was developing around particular features of being a State Enterprise, namely lack of funding, political uncertainty, changing priorities, and a rigid, bureaucratic structure. At this point, I held meetings with the ARG in order to share and discuss my initial findings, and to collectively agree on and plan action. Although the first three meetings generated agreed actions, they also surfaced more factors with implications for the organisation's delivery of customer care and its capacity to improve.

For staff, the ARG meetings were an unusual opportunity to speak freely and candidly about their experience of the organisation. Many staff expressed longstanding frustrations with the many failed change interventions in the organisation. There was open blaming and even name calling of other Departments and their failures to act and communicate effectively (something that I emphasised was not appropriate in a multi-Departmental group). Senior management was seen as remote and separate and frequently referred to as "them".

One significant moment occurred early on in the first meeting when staff asked for clarification as to whether being part of the group was voluntary and whether their time spent in the group would form part of their key performance indicators. This spoke to a culture of command and control where staff felt that they were only valued and recognised if they were complying with pre-determined rules. It also related to a wider observation that if staff was to deliver good customer care, then the organisation needed to take care of its employees. Staff also corroborated much of my initial diagnosis. Departmental silos were highlighted, and staff noted that the publicness and funding constraints might mean having to differentiate between tenant needs and wants, and being able to prioritise the former. Staff also reported that process changes were poorly communicated, both vertically and between Departments which eventually created bottlenecks in trying to progress tenant complaints.

Given that no inquiry is context free (Coghlan and Casey, 2001) and there are many explanations for organisational brokenness, I was interested in hearing the many versions of the story and allowed all the voices of the group members to be heard. What was also noticeable, within the staff expressions of frustration, was that they consistently referred to tenants as customers, in contrast to corporate strategic documents and the executive interviewees.

By the second and third meetings, I was able to focus the meetings on identifying principles of good customer care. Based on their own experiences, the group agreed on principles of improved communication and commitment, professionalism, respect, active listening to customers' needs and equity in treatment.

The group agreed that its main goal was to write a policy document for customer care which embedded the principles they had identified. However, the group also agreed that before they started to write it, feedback from the entire organisation should be sought on customer care delivery.

Applying Action Research: Taking action

A questionnaire was developed with input from the ARG and issued to all staff via the company's intranet. The purpose of the questionnaire was to generate data as to whether RESL was viewed as being customer centric or not, whether clear goals around customer care existed and if the company was meeting the customers' needs. There were 18 responses from 74 staff members.

The group analysed the responses. A key headline was that 61% of the respondents disagreed that the company had clearly defined goals and targets focused on improving customer service. Qualitative comments revealed several common issues. The first was that organisational processes relating to customer care were perceived to be inadequate or broken. Respondents commented that the organisation had neither "follow up with internal and external customers" nor provided "simple feedback when customers want responses to queries" and that there was too much focus on bureaucracy or "procrastination with paper work."

Some staff identified problems with staff attitudes: "We do not have the right mind set or the right attitude. Staff are not willing to go the extra mile to satisfy our internal and external stakeholders." Some staff expressed frustration that the company was not enabling them to do what they felt their roles required: "As an employee I recognize that customer care is vital to the service we provide, and within the organization I haven't seen any focus on this area."

Reflecting on the findings thus far, I concluded that my most effective strategy for taking action and engendering change would be ongoing engagement from the bottom up, within my own personal span of control as a Departmental manager. This included continuing to facilitate the group meetings as a space for catharsis as well as staff input and insight. All evidence to date suggested that the focus of executive management rested with capital works on the industrial properties in accordance with the company's mandate as handed down by the Government, and would continue to be so.

The findings from the questionnaire helped to confirm the content of the workplan agreed by the group. This comprised two major elements: the development of a Customer Care Policy, and a Complaints Handling process. The company had never completed a Customer Care Policy to communicate the company's principles, practices and service standards in customer care and complaints handling due to changing demands as dictated by executive management. All members of the ARG were assigned responsibilities for writing different sections of the Policy, based on the customer care principles agreed within the group, with clear timelines for completion.

Feedback from the staff survey and discussions within the group had also highlighted many broken areas along the customer journey. The company had no mechanism to electronically generate and share work order numbers with a tenant or the originating Department in order to be updated on work process or closure of a work order. In acknowledging the tenant's issue, it was not possible to advise the tenant as to how long it would take to have an issue such as roof repairs rectified as, in most instances, it was a function of available funding. In the language of the organisation, there was no clear definition of what was considered a complaint.

Any issues raised by tenants involving bricks and mortar were labelled as maintenance issues. In revising and implementing the complaints process, the group examined all customer touch points, developed additional documentation to track complaints, refined response times and leveraged technology, whereby all complaints were logged using SharePoint and forwarded to the respective Officer in the Maintenance Department for action.

Within the Department where I served as Manager, I introduced a tenant site visit verification initiative, whereby once a tenant was visited by a technical officer from the team, a follow up call was made to the tenant in order to assess the quality of customer care delivery. The outcome of the interview would be documented and communicated to the Manager for further discussion. The Tenants' Portal on the company's website was also revamped as another avenue to allow tenants to document issues and concerns, coupled with the reintroduction of a tenants' hotline.

Applying Action Research: Evaluating action

Reflecting on the actions taken, I am of the view that my original constructing of RESL's problem was accurate. The data generated throughout the action cycle based on different sources have highlighted both the organisational problem of poor customer care at this State Enterprise and the many aspects of publicness that hinder a sustained focus on and implementation of customer care. The actions taken alongside the ARG were in line with the construction of the problem, as the heart of the problem rested with the fact that as a SPSE, the company was more focused on the completion of capital projects and development of new industrial sites for leasing. Little to no focus was placed on strengthening the landlord-tenant relationship.

As part of my work with the ARG I was able to develop a Customer Care Policy and a Customer Complaints Handling Process. No documented Customer Care Policy or complaints process existed in the company before, and as such, the Policy was the first step in placing focus on how RESL was expected to deliver customer care.

The complaints handling process which enabled relevant Departments to track tenants' complaints in real time in order to update them on the status of their matters, was successfully implemented. However, organisational approval of the Customer

Care Policy was subject to a lengthy process to put it on the agenda of the company's Board of Directors. I exited the organisation in 2020, by which time the policy still had not received approval.

Discussion: Change from below

The action research study was undertaken in order to understand, firstly, why attempts to improve customer care and customer relationship management at RESL continued to fail; and secondly, what actions are required to embed customer care policies and practices within RESL. The undertaking of one macro cycle of Action Research, with the full participation of an ARG representing staff from multiple Departments, has generated valuable insights into both questions.

The reasons why attempts to improve customer care and customer relationship management continued to fail are myriad. As I had suspected from my own managerial experience, they all related to the public nature of RESL as a Special Purpose State Enterprise. The collection and analysis of multiple data sources including corporate strategic documents, tenant surveys, staff surveys, tenant records, executive interviews and action research group discussions revealed that many different aspects and consequences of publicness were at play.

As a State Enterprise, RESL was mandated to become commercially viable and as such, experienced a consequent reduction of state funding. The company remained subject to political influence and the five-year political cycle, meaning that changing political priorities and short-term goals continued to dominate, rather than long term investment and strategic change. One of the important things that was learned was that despite incorporating the language of customer relationship management within strategic documents, practices throughout RESL continued to assume a transactional landlord-tenant relationship. Based on the language of the organisation, there was no holistic view of the customer as tenant because different Departments saw themselves as responsible for only one aspect of the tenant's business.

Culturally, RESL remained highly bureaucratic and process focused, with Departments fixated on their own discrete span of control rather than collective responsibility. From the perspective of practice, customer complaints were not systematically managed, but reacted to, mainly when the tenant pursued it, and they were primarily treated as maintenance tasks.

The findings, particularly from the diagnostic stage of the action research cycle reflect much of the literature on the challenges of implementing effective CRM, including the need for a strategic approach (Boakye-Agyeman and Bugri, 2019; Gibson ,2006; Wojewnik-Filipkowska et al., 2015), integrated and cross-functional systems for customer relationship management (Haynes and Haynes, 2012; Kumar, 2012; Lalloo, 2013; Rababah et al., 2011), and the need for sustained top management commitment (Bibiano, 2014; Farhan et al. 2018; Kumar, 2012; Mohd et.al 2011; Tekin ,2013). The findings further reflect particular challenges from a practical perspective for public sector landlords including differences between a landlord-tenant and a business-customer relationship (Hanis et al., 2011; Kaganova and Nayyar-Stone, 2000; Kivlehan, 2011), the tensions between public and private sector paradigms (Buttle & Maklan, 2019; Fountain, 2001; Thomas, 2013), and the challenges of being a 'quasi-public' or 'social business' (Collier, 2005; Gruis & Nieboer, 2004). Understanding why attempts to implement and improve customer care in RESL had continued to fail, the biggest insight was seeing how these many challenges all played out, and mutually reinforced each other within the organisation.

The conclusions from the diagnosis phase of the action research cycle were not only that the change needed at RESL to effectively implement and sustain customer relationship management was multiple and complex, but that there were many constraining factors, including a lack of funding and a lack of top management commitment due to the public nature of the SPSE. Undertaking action research also revealed scope to begin to enact change 'from below' as Managers such as the lead author can and do have influence in their organisation both through their span of control over resources and people, and through their personal behaviours.

The lead author also found that there was considerable support amongst members of the ARG and other staff for improving customer care and for changing their own practices, such as working more co-operatively across Departments. The ARG was able to collectively write a draft Customer Care Policy, design and implement a Complaints Handling Process owned by the lead author's Department but supported by others. This activity was a significant breakthrough as neither had previously been achieved despite many previous attempts.

The action research therefore offers an important insight into the practice of customer relationship management and its organisational implementation. Although the literature emphasises the importance of top management commitment and the organisation-wide integration of people, processes and technology to create a customer-centric organisation (Rababah et al., 2011), this paper also illustrates that meaningful change is not dependent on top management support. In reality, customer care can be improved by working at a local level where people, processes and technology can be co-ordinated and where there is commitment to cross- functionality (Kumar and Reinartz, 2018) which incorporates the needs of the tenant in a seamless manner.

Reflections after action: the lead author's experience

> As I undertook the action research project, I was mindful of who I was vis-à-vis the research process. My positionality in the organisation as a long-standing Manager and now insider action researcher brought with it considerable practical and technical considerations that I tried to manage carefully and not become narcissistic (Weick, 2002).
>
> Throughout the phases, I questioned my beliefs and understanding of the core problem. As a change agent, I reflected on myself as well as the ARG and the context for the proposed activities. This reflection led to active agency

in terms of identifying the core problem as well as recognising the challenges ahead given my span of control.

I acknowledged the possible conflict which could have arisen given my role complexity as researcher and employee. I was conscious that I brought to the inquiry my values, experiences and perceptions about the organisation.

Manoeuvring between my role as insider action researcher and Manager was challenging given my knowledge of the organisation, nevertheless I allowed my thoughts about the situation to be reframed as the research progressed.

Reflecting on all the actions taken throughout the macro action research cycle, I did not achieve all that I wanted to achieve and had to work from the bottom up as the attention of executive management was focused on capital works to develop new industrial properties for leasing.

What I learned about myself was that as an insider action researcher, in order to survive and thrive, I had to be patient with myself, mindful of the organisational dynamics that go with Government institutions such as RESL. Advancement of the inquiry required me to jump into the fray to curb the blame game which had the potential to derail progress. In those circumstances, in order to survive, I took on the role of Manager and not insider action researcher resulting in me shifting between identities.

The outcome for the organisation as evidenced by employees having a better appreciation for excellent customer care delivery was achieved. As a start, the Customer Care Policy was completed and forwarded to executive management. The customer complaints handling process was revised and integrated as part of the Division's work flow process in collaboration with the Maintenance Department. The sustainability of the customer complaints handling process required close monitoring of the process, as change requires people to embrace new processes, practices and behaviours which make them uncomfortable. At the centre of change is the people element which can either spell failure or success for any change initiative. I reflected on and in the action which took place and I tried to not transfer my feelings to the members of the group.

What I learned about management practice and change management is that for any organisational change to occur, one has to develop an enquiring approach and challenge existing organisational processes to achieve improved organisational performance and productivity. It is possible for these improvements to occur 'from below' as demonstrated in this action research thesis, once participants are allowed to give voice to their concerns.

Conclusions

Central to the survivability of any business is the strength of customer relationships. This includes public sector organisations, especially as they become increasingly subject to NPM prescriptions and are expected to become financially self-sustainable. This paper has presented an action research project undertaken by the lead author in a Caribbean Special Purpose State Enterprise, RESL, which is landlord to over 300 light manufacturing tenants. The project aimed to address the longstanding tenant dissatisfaction with RESL, which often manifested in withheld rent. It aimed to investigate firstly, why attempts to improve customer care and customer relationship management at RESL have continued to fail; and secondly, the actions required to embed customer care policies and practices within RESL.

The research found that the public nature of RESL impacted significantly on its ability to focus on customer care, as well as a lack of funding, a bureaucratic structure, reliance on processes, and its continuing dependency on political influence and the political cycle. There remained a disconnect between how the organisation spoke about tenants as customers within its Strategic Plan, successive launches of customer care strategies, and how it dealt transactionally with tenants in practice. The company can be defined as a Model I company. In Model I companies, there is a disconnect between what Argyris and Schön (1997) defined as 'theories espoused' and 'theories in use'. What was needed, therefore, was not first and second order change whereby old ways of thinking about customer care remained, but third order change which challenged the culture and practices of the organisation.

As Manager and inside action researcher, my vested interest in the company was the impetus to drive change from below and reposition the Department to one focused on customer care. Although I was unable to effect change at the executive or strategic level, as a result of my role as an action researcher, I was able to achieve the outcome of changed procedures in the Department to the benefit of the company. The value derived from the action research project was the ability to engage in a rigorous investigative process to improve organisational practice and policy. The process resulted in the development of new knowledge directly related to the organisation through the collection and analysis of data which led to decision making on customer care and complaints handling.

There is a paucity of research on CRM in the public sector in the Caribbean, moreso public sector organisations that are landlords who depend on lease rents as their source of revenue. The evidence from this study provides a clearer understanding of the challenges of implementing CREM in a Special Purpose State Enterprise, and especially the challenges of implementing CRM practices. It highlights the multiple effects of publicness including lack of funding, a bureaucratic structure and reliance on processes. There is also continuing dependency on political influence, and effects including organisational inertia, employee disengagement and push-back. The value of a case study such as this is a demonstration of the effects of multiple factors, and the challenge for the individual manager in effecting change. It reveals, through a 'bottom-up' perspective, why implementing a customer-focused culture and supporting processes in a public organisation can be so hard, and why so many such programmes fail, as they did at RESL.

The paper also offers a contribution to management practice. Through the research, the lead author was able to create meaningful change within her organisation despite the lack of top management support. The intervention challenged the policies and procedures of the company and drove change through co-opting staff who also sought to see change themselves and to be part of it. A particular, sometimes undervalued benefit of action research, is its ability to enable a manager, as an insider researcher, to step back from the day-to-day organisational rhetoric and to listen and give voice to different organisational members. This desire was evident at action research group meetings where members expressed the view that they experienced too many unsuccessful change initiatives due to the way the change was implemented. At an action research group meeting, one participant opined that "the level of efficiency and follow up with internal and external customers is lacking." Whilst another expressed the view that "simple feedback when customers want responses to queries is not developed." Capacity was therefore built amongst members of the ARG, as the change process was not foisted upon them. Their voices were integral to how change was planned and implemented. With the development of a Customer Care Policy and complaints handling process, the foundation was set for RESL to deliver a better level of service to its customers.

Future work

The focus of this inquiry was to gain a better understanding of the challenges of embedding CRM and customer care in RESL. In the light of the findings from the study and key conclusions, from a policy perspective there is the need for future research into how SPSEs such as RESL can surmount five-year political cycles and insulate the organisation to ensure sustainability of projects.

With the recognition that public sector real estate has placed little focus on customer centricity, an unresolved question of managerial practice is how this sector can incorporate customer value at the center of organisational decision making despite competing demands, and the threat of reduced funding. This unresolved issue calls for in-depth research into the most appropriate method of engagement to realise a hybrid top down and bottom-up approach between landlord and tenant. This engagement can assist in arriving at a consensus on the value that the landlord will provide and what the tenant expects to receive. Following on from this point will be the need for research to quantify the financial return to landlords as evidenced by better performing real estate assets should they embrace the hybrid approach to creating customer value.

References

Abraham, S. (2012) *Work-applied learning for change*. Australia, AIB Publications Pty Ltd.

Argyris, C., & Schön, D. A. (1997) Organizational learning: A theory of action perspective. Reis, no. 77/78, pp. 345-48. JSTOR, https://doi.org/10.2307/40183951 (Accessed 30 January 2023).

Bibiano, L. H., Marco-Simó, J. M. & Pastor, J. A. (2014) An initial approach for improving CRM systems implementation projects, *CISTI* (Iberian Conference on Information Systems & Technologies / Conferência Ibérica de Sistemas e Tecnologias de Informação) *Proceedings*, 1, pp. 118-123. Available at: https://search-ebscohost-com.liverpool.idm.oclc.org/login.aspx?direct=true&db=iih&AN=97081294&site=eds-live&scope=site (Accessed: 27 April 2020).

Boakye-Agyeman, N.A. & Bugri, J.T. (2019) Strategic corporate real estate management practice in Ghana. *Property Management*. 37 (3), pp. 432-449.

Buttle, F. & Maklan, S. (2019) *Customer relationship management: concepts and technologies*. Routledge.

Coghlan, D. & Casey, M. (2001) Action research from the inside: issues and challenges in doing action research in your own hospital. *Journal of Advanced Nursing*. 35 (5), pp. 674-682.

Coghlan, D. & Brannick, T. (2010) *Doing action research in your own organization*. 3rd ed. London, Sage Publications.

Collier, P. M. (2005) Governance and the quasi-public organisation: A case study of social housing. *Critical Perspectives on Accounting*. 16 (7), 929-949.

Creswell, J. (2013) *Qualitative inquiry and research design: choosing among five approaches*. 3rd ed. London, Sage Publications.

Edwards, V. & Ellison, L. (2004) *Corporate property management – Aligning real estate with business strategy*. Blackwell Publishing Company.

Farhan, M.S., Abed, A.H. & Ellatif, M.A. (2018). A systematic review for the determination and classification of the CRM critical success factors supporting with their metrics. *Future Computing and Informatics Journal.* 3 (2), pp. 398-416.

Fountain, J. (2001) Paradoxes of public sector customer service. *Governance: An International Journal of Policy and Administration.* 14 (1), pp. 55-73.

Gibson, V. (2006) Is property on the strategic agenda? *ACES Spring Conference.* Bath, May 2006. Paper No. 06.5/2, pp. 13-20.

Gruis, V., & Nieboer, N. (2004) Market orientation in social housing management. *Property Management.* 22 (3), 186-188.

Hanis, M.H., Trigunarsyah, B. & Susilawati, C. (2011) The application of public asset management in Indonesian local government: A case study in South Sulawesi province. *Journal of Corporate Real Estate.* 13 (1), 36-47.

Haynes, B. & Haynes, B.P. (2012) Corporate real estate asset management: aligned vision. *Journal of Corporate Real Estate.* 14 (4), 244-254.

Heywood, C. (2011) Approaches to aligning corporate real estate and organisational strategy. In: *Proceedings of the 18th European Real Estate Society Conference,* 15-18 June Eindhoven, The Netherlands, pp. 1-15.

Hsiao, Y.H., Chen, L.F., Choy, Y.L. & Su, C.T. (2016) A novel framework for customer complaint management. *The Service Industries Journal,* 36 (13-14), 675-698.

Johnson, P. & Duberley, J. (2012) *Understanding management research. An introduction to epistemology.* London, Sage Publications.

Kaganova, O. & Nayyar-Stone, R. (2000)'Municipal real property asset management: An overview of world experience, trends and financial implications. *Journal of Real Estate Portfolio Management.* 6 (4) 307-326.

Kask, K. (2014) *Public sector real estate asset management models and their evaluation* (Doctoral dissertation), University of Tartu, Estonia.

King, N. & Horrocks, C. 2010 *Interviews in qualitative research.* London, UK, Sage.

Kivlehan, N. P. (2011) What's in a name? *Estates Gazette.* Issue 1109, pp. 78-80.

Kumar V. (2012) Strategic customer relationship management today. In: *Customer Relationship Management. Springer Texts in Business and Economics.* Berlin, Heidelberg, Springer. https://doi.org/10.1007/978-3-642-20110-3_1, pp. 3-20.

Kumar V. & Reinartz W. (2018) Strategic CRM today. In: *Customer Relationship Management. Springer Texts in Business and Economics.*

Berlin, Heidelberg, Springer. https://doi.org/10.1007/978-3-662-55381-7_1, pp. 3-16.

Lalloo, A. (2013) *Corporate real estate practices in South Africa: A survey of the top 200 companies listed on the Johannesburg stock exchange*. (Doctoral dissertation) University of the Witwatersrand, Faculty of Engineering and the Built Environment.

Marona, B. (2016) Public management in a real estate area – Some empirical evidence from Polish municipalities. *Real Estate Management and Valuation*, 24 (4), pp. 16-22.

Mohd, H., Rababah, K., & Ibrahim, H. (2011) Critical success factors (CSFS) of the pre-adoption and pre-implementation plan of Customer Relationship Management (CRM) system. *Proceedings of the 3rd International Conference on Computing and Informatics*, ICOCI 2011, 8-9 June, 2011 Bandung, Indonesia, pp. 266-272.

Palm, P. (2011) Customer orientation in real-estate companies: The espoused values of customer relations. *Journal of Property Management*, 29 (2), pp. 130-145.

Pareja, A., Fernández, C., Blanco, B., Theobald, K., & Martínez, A. (2016) *Simplifying lives: Quality and satisfaction in public services*. [Online] https://publications.iadb.org/en/simplifying-lives-quality-and-satisfaction-public-services (Accessed 10 April 2020).

Rababah, K., Mohd, H., & Ibrahim, H. (2011) Processes from theory to practice: The pre-implementation plan of CRM system. *International Journal of e-Education, e-Business, e-Management and e-Learning* 1 (1), 22-27.

Saunders, M., Lewis, P. & Thornhill, A. (2016) *Research methods for business students*. England, Pearson Education Limited.

Smith, T.A. & Charles, C.A. (2018) A decomposed CKM model for better explaining customer satisfaction in the Jamaican public sector. *International Journal of Public Sector Performance Management*, 4 (4), 411-432.

Stauss, B. & Seidel, W. (2019) *Effective complaint management: The business case for customer satisfaction*. Springer.

Sulaiman, N.N., Diah, M.L.M., Ramin, A., Omar, A.J. & Ambar, A. (2015) Corporate real estate performance in Malaysian Public Listed companies. In: *21st annual Pacific-rim real estate society conference*, 18-21 January, Kuala Lumpur, Malaysia, pp. 1-12.

Tekin, M. (2013) Critical Success Factors for a Customer Relationship Management Strategy. *Mediterranean Journal of Social Sciences*. 4 (10), 753. Retrieved from https://www.mcser.org/journal/index.php/mjss/article/view/1258 (Accessed 27 April 2020).

Thomas, J.C. (2013) Citizen, customer, partner: Rethinking the place of the public in public management. *Public Administration Review*. 73 (6), 786-796.

van den Beemt-Tjeerdsma, A. & Veuger, J. (2016) Towards a more professionalised municipal real estate management. *Journal of Corporate Real Estate*, 18 (2), 132-144.

Weick, K.E. (2002) Real time reflexivity: prods to reflection. *Organisation Studies*, 23 (6), 893-898.

Wojewnik-Filipkowska, A., Rymarzak, M. & Lausberg, C., 2015 Current managerial topics in public real estate asset management. *World of Real Estate*. 4 (94), 5-10.

Biography

Dr. Erica Prentice has more than 14 years' experience working in a senior managerial position in a Special Purpose State Enterprise (SPSE) in the Caribbean. Her background in landlord and tenant matters was gained through work at the SPSE. This led to the topic for her action research Doctoral thesis on CRM and the challenges in engendering change from below.

A graduate of the University of Liverpool, she is a MBA Lecturer at SITAL College of Tertiary Education.

Her research interests include strategic management and the alignment between real estate and business strategy within the context of corporate property management.

Dr Ali Rostron is a Senior Lecturer at the University of Liverpool Management School and a Senior Fellow of the Higher Education Academy. She works on a range of international postgraduate programmes including the Doctorate of Business Administration. Before academia, Ali spent many years as a manager in the charity sector and local government. Her research focuses on manager identity, education and development, examined particularly through narrative and autoethnography, and has been published in Management Learning and the Journal of Management Inquiry.

"Hunchifactuality": Identifying and alleviating bias with pragmatic action research

Jack Brady

Abstract

This paper discusses how a pragmatic action research (AR) strategy assisted to identify researcher bias and positively influenced participant recruitment during my PhD project in Political Science. I started by recruiting participants through traditional text-based methods based on limited definitions of satire (see Condren, 2012; Phiddian, 2020) rather than more informal, practice based conversations at key annual festival events. My project aimed to locate and centre Australian comedians performing political and/or social justice inspired comedy as a potential form of political expression. I had both insider and outsider positionality (as both a comedian who did social justice inspired comedy and an anthropologist). In my recruitment practice I mistook my bias towards traditional knowledge production for rigour and dismissed hunches that would later prove to be valuable practice-led insights. This unconscious bias in my recruitment practice was revealed by initial recruitment failures, which were remedied by revisiting the core practice-led tenant of pragmatic AR.

Key words: Political expression, pragmatic action research, bias, positionality, comedy, satire, cultural democracy, representation, anthropology, political science

What is known about the topic?

Arieli, Friedman, & Agbaria (2009) discusses the paradox of participation in action research. Friedman & Rogers (2009) discusses the challenges of theory and knowledge reproduction in action research. Greenwood (2007) has discussed pragmatic action research to work with the needs of specific groups. Lenette (2022) discusses the potential and limitations of action research as a decolonising methodology.

What does this paper add?

This article discusses a PhD researcher's account of the participatory challenges of unacknowledged bias when recruiting participants for researchers with insider or dual insider/outsider positionality. It examines how centring practice-led and pragmatic action research principles can be used to assist researcher assessments of their biases.

Who will benefit from its content?

- AR seminar facilitators in a university or community-based setting
- Community engaged researchers and scholars interested in action research
- Students of AR
- AR dissertation writers

What is the relevance to AL and AR scholars and practitioners?

- The significance of Pragmatic AR design to research over 12 months to 24 months in duration
- Ways of managing research when there are increasing cross-disciplinary or multidisciplinary demands for rigour
- Discussion of interest-based communities and how action research can be mobilised when participants are geographically or socially diffuse but share practices in common

Received   October 2024   Reviewed   November 2024   Published   December 2024

Introduction: Project Planning, Insider Positionality, Hunches and Bias.

My PhD project, 'You Can't Laugh at That! The Politics of Australian Political Comedy' (currently in pre-submission edits) consisted of three methods within a pragmatic AR strategy. The research question relates to whether popular mainstream forms of Australian political satire maintain the social status quo in terms of the representation of diversity. The AR fieldwork aimed to centre the voices of grassroots comedians and their content moderation practices. I was aware that my initial planning for fieldwork was based upon the presumption of an easily defined community of participants, as comedians who perform political satire. Drawing from my insider positionality I knew comedians did not fit a traditional research definition of a community, even though it was common to hear the expression "comedy community" in backstage conversation.

In the first year of my PhD, I found myself in an intensive action research course with Dr Akihiro Ogawa and wondering if action research would help alleviate my positionality concerns. During that action research intensive, I realised I had been an accidental action researcher as an applied anthropologist for 15 years. I concluded that I needed to refine experiences such as facilitating homelessness action groups into my PhD project using problem-based interviewing. Problem based interviewing techniques centre what practitioners think is the problem and work backwards from their assessment of problem areas, rather than working from the researchers assessment of the problem. However, I was planning fieldwork from a position of worry about affinity or confirmation bias or what Brewis (2014) calls 'convenience sampling'. After the initial failures to recruit, the renewed recruitment strategy based on pragmatic, practice-led recruitment allowed for the meaningful contribution of 29 participants; with only 4 of them individuals I knew. I was also concerned about disciplinary bias, to avoid too much reliance on ethnographic methods (as an anthropologist engaged in a political science PhD). My initial recruitment efforts were designed around text-based, linear recruitment methods rather than ongoing observation-based recruitment and were not very effective.

I consulted with Dr Ogawa, who urged me to look more closely at my design and what I needed to do to ensure it was a pragmatic AR strategy. Revising my approach to get back to pragmatic AR principles allowed me to acknowledge an unconscious bias that prioritised theoretical broad definitions of satire over my own valid experience and hunches that came from my dual insider/outsider positionality. Greenwood (2007, p. 131, my emphasis) describes pragmatic AR is 'a strategy for research that self-consciously and strategically combines multiple methods and techniques *according to the concrete needs of particular groups and situations'*. Revisiting those words helped me get back to the work of centring what comedians valued, rather than unnecessary worry about bias. Rather than see bias as something to be avoided, I needed to acknowledge the potential for unconscious bias; but also rethink how my "hunches" might be valid and important to communication and collaboration in any research (Covitt & Anderson, 2022; Lin, 2023).

The renewed recruitment approach abandoned broad theoretical definitions of satire and text-based traditional recruitment methods. Instead, I focussed on conversations about the politics of comedy at events, emphasising the one constant, or concrete need for comedians, which was annual festivals. This allowed ongoing recruitment of participants. This more pragmatic approach was more in keeping with my experience in my applied anthropology career before PhD study. In hindsight, much of that work was based on the neo-pragmatism of the non-for-profit world of remote Australia. Rather than be on one singular project, an anthropologist may have to stretch themselves over a range of community contexts in short times. This is consistent with the neo-pragmatism of pragmatic AR which requires a 'purposive design of the projects to enhance co-generative learning while they are in the process is the core principle of practice' (Greenwood and Levin, 2007, p. 2). A shift from trying to conceptualise a comedy community, offset bias and positionality concerns to a pragmatic AR focus on events such as festivals allowed comedians to better contribute to the study at 'the conjunction of three elements: action, research, and participation' (Greenwood & Levin, 2007, p. 6).

Australian comedians operate sporadically in a nebulous, geographically dispersed, interest-based, and personally diverse arts environment. Comedy production is competitive and stretched across different genres, styles, and forms of comedy, with Melbourne, Australia, arguably positioned as comedy's heartland. As an anthropologist (and occasional comedian), I tend to see community in everything and everywhere. So, I took the approach that even school or hospital environments may grant access to participants as part of a community of shared interests, a 'school community' for example, so I assumed this description would suffice for comedians.

On this basis, my initial plans for recruiting participants had begun as though the comedy community was a geographic or ethnicity-based community with a sub-group called satirists. This need to offset affinity or confirmation bias, had become my bias, placing traditional knowledge paradigms hierarchically over and above the communities interests. It also meant I ignored my hunches about Australian comedian resistance to the word satire. Hunches can be simply described as reasonable estimations of behaviour based on researcher experience (for a more complex description see Lin, 2023). In the first few weeks of fieldwork, I failed to recruit because I was using theoretical sampling instead of practice-led AR principles, and had to reset the project and effectively, start again. This paper discusses how revisiting the practical in a pragmatic AR strategy allows acknowledgement of positionality, bias and encourages a rethink of insider hunches as potentially useful (something I call *hunchifactuality*).

The 'You Can't Laugh at That' project examined comedian decision-making about self-censorship and content moderation as indicators of the processes and logics of comedy production as potential political expression (Cook & Heilmann, 2013; Sparrow, 2024). This was considered relative to any socio-political barriers between mainstream high-profile comedians to grassroots[1] community-based comedians. Australian comedy sits alongside the symbolic expression of national and personal identities and acts as a mirror to the social status quo of the time (Higgie, 2013;

---

1   For this research, *grassroots* satirists/comedians are defined as those who have smaller public profiles and for whom most of their income will come from sources other than comedy and satire, but who remain committed to their craft over several years and can produce shows of more an hour duration. Mainstream refers to comedians with larger national and/or international level public profiles where it could be said comedy provides most of their income.

Knowles, 2022). One of the most often discussed forms of Australian comedy is the often-lighter *larrikin* model of Australian comedy. The larrikin has a long history, from the early 1800s colonial rogue who ran anti-authoritarian street gangs called a 'push' through to post-1960s less violent examples of someone who is likeable but provocative in their cultural criticism (Rickard, 1998). The larrikin comedian is more likely to say things that are not used in polite conversation or to touch on social taboos in their work, but some scholars argue this can be politically superficial (Cothren & Phiddian, 2019; Holm, 2017; Milner Davis & Foyle, 2017). However, as my research is located with political science, the research also relates to how comedian activities might respond relative to government scrutiny, funding, and policy over time.

To give further context to the learnings in this paper, it's important to first explain the research topic in relation to the use of overidentification satire (or authentic irony)[2] as political expression. What this research calls overidentification satire comes from a technique in satire that mocks reality closely (sometimes described as authentic irony) that is linked to the post-Soviet *stiob* (Day, 2011; Boyer & Yurchak, 2010). It's also closely aligned with firsthand experiences and people using comedy to relate the experiences of oppressed groups (Yurcak, 2006). Overidentification satire was selected as the basis of the PhD project as a more activist and personal form of satire (see also Bogad, 2005), to look for its presence in Australia and for any political expression implications for comedians.

A historical approach is taken in the research to help map over time to what extent contemporary grassroots[3] comedy might

---

2. There were themes in the research that possibly could allow for another category of authentic irony, that I would consider lived experience irony. However, I am cautious about how I use this language for the connection to medical or mental health paradigms. While I discuss lived experience throughout this paper, I reserve that for comedian personal experience, and overidentification satire for the use of their lived experience in their comedy.

3. For this research, grassroots satirists/comedians are defined as those who have smaller public profiles and for whom most of their income will come from

challenge older forms of political comedy (such as the larrikin model) as it relates to political expression (Kavanagh, 1991). The chosen form of overidentification satire is linked to post-Soviet forms of satire that reflected the lived experience of oppression during periods of rapid social and political change (Boyer & Yurchak, 2010; Yurchak, 2006). Effectively, overidentification satire targets governments and social institutions relative to the experience of oppression in more subtle ways than other forms of satire. However, despite wanting to be practice-led (which means I should focus on comedic practice that was more subtle) I chose to use the broader explicit definition of satire or political comedy in the recruitment materials. These initial recruitment errors represented unconscious bias to overcompensate for traditional methodological concerns about sampling convenience, instead of centring comedian practice.

One of the other unexpected outcomes of this process of rethinking recruitment in practice-led ways, was it allowed two AR cycles, and it attracted greater numbers of and more diverse participants. This layering of methods assisted in the ongoing recruitment of 29 participants and rich quality data collection, assisted to unpack positionality concerns and trust building. Paying close attention to my positionality helped uncover any biases and manage the power dynamics and the subsequent explicit conversations with comedians allowed for trust building. I was also, in these conversations, acknowledging that research is inherently political (Friedman & Rogers, 2009; Greenwood, 2002; Herr & Anderson, 2005; Ogawa, 2006).

---

sources other than comedy and satire, but who remain committed to their craft over several years and actively engaged in yearly festival presentations and solo shows of more an hour duration. Mainstream or popular is used to describe comedians who have larger (usually national and/or international) public profiles where it could be said most of their income comes from comedy or other creative products related to comedy.

'To Satire or Not to Satire:' Hunches, Bias, and the Positionality Spectrum

The main source of unconscious bias was I was depending on too broad definitions of satire to recruit (see figure 1) prior to observation or interviewing. I knew that theoretically what I was looking for was comedians in the Australian comedy community who are best described as satirists (Holm, 2017; Phiddian, 2017, 2020). But the key aspect of the hunch that had allowed me to write the PhD proposal was that comedians might avoid being seen as satirists or political, and it might mirror the political expression environment in Australia (Dawson & Brady, 2021). This hunch was proved to have some merit as there was an apparent lack of interest in my study with several comedians commenting "I don't do satire."

I knew that conceptualising comedians as a singular community was also problematic, for more political comedians could be engaged in behaviours consistent with movements of resistance and persistence (Fox, 2017, 2018). Members of this community come from varied backgrounds, but it is no secret comedians from marginalised communities are often excluded from mainstream platforms such as national TV (Brookfield, 2019; Sless, 2022; Fox 2017, 2018). Some participants discussed how grassroots comedy is often not deemed suitable for mainstream audiences or media consumption by TV executives and large media outlets. While there is an overarching commitment to making audiences laugh, comedians tend to operate autonomously or in smaller groups and organise in a geographically and socially diffuse manner.

Additionally, economic pressures on the hospitality and entertainment industry mean that the way comedians navigate turning an interest into a profession is challenging. This includes the casualisation of labour and fewer formal arts work opportunities (Throsby & Zednik, 2010; Throsby & Petetskaya, 2024). However, when I've talked to other comedians, they do acknowledge shared difficulties and passions that you might expect within other communities based on geographic, ethnic, or

Anthropologist and PhD researcher Jack Brady is looking for comedians and satirists to take part in a study on the social and political pressures placed upon Australian comedy production. There are performance opportunities (with associated honorarium fee paid to you) as well as interview opportunities.

This project will make an important contribution to the understanding of the political pressures upon Australian comedy and satire production and the Australian arts industries and begin conversations about the safekeeping of satirical and artistic political commentary.

Places are limited and you don't have to be a political satirist (just have an interest in social issues in your content across any range of topics), so if you are interested, please send an email to jack.brady1@student.unimelb.edu.au with a few lines about your comedy background as an expression of interest by the XX XXX 20XX.

Figure 1. Recruitment advert for email and Facebook

occupational proximity. Like Charmaz's (2014) work with people from diverse backgrounds sharing their experiences with the medical system, comedians share a sense of community from their shared experiences producing comedy in the entertainment industry. My informal conversations, in the years before formal research, informed my hunch[4] that comedians are not united by community per se, but by shared values about a particular form[5] of comedy.

Yet I would go onto to attempt to recruit based upon my own insistence in using broadly theoretical descriptions of satire (ignored my hunch). I then spent more time than necessary to find comedians willing to participate. In addressing the lack of participants, I shifted back to emphasising that specific overidentification techniques were what I was interested in, not satire. My initial broad recruitment strategy dismissed my hunch about comedians being evasive around notions of satire even if performing comedy that could be described as such.

I've coined the word *hunchifactuality* (a combination of hunch and factuality); to describe this process of discerning what part of my initial recruitment strategy ignored valuable lived experience and observation for fear it was bias or convenience sampling. I wanted to offset this hunch about aversion to the word satire with recruiting materials that used the word satire, instead of a finer grained description of practice. I emphasised the word satire,

---

4   Generally, a hunch is a feeling that might or might not be proved later by evidence (Lin, 2023). It is not the intent of this paper to go in depth into what is and isn't a hunch. Except to say that I was overly concerned with empiricism and not taking my lived experience of ten years into account as both potential bias and valuable to the research.

5   There are various genres, and most sources argue the number of genres ranging from 20 to over 60. Examples include dark (about topics like death), blue (sexual content), slapstick (features physical acts like falling over). It's important to stress that the PhD research is not theatre studies or communication but political science and references to genre and form are simplified as a result.

which to comedians was a theoretical distinction, not a practice-based distinction.

After the initial failed attempts at recruitment (in the first eight weeks), a renewed pragmatic and festival focussed recruitment strategy found that the participants avoided the word satire in the promotion of their work. This came from face-to-face interactions at festivals, after little interest in emails, Facebook posts and several comedians telling me they were not satirists, I realised I should have paid more attention to my hunch. However, all was not lost, and the theoretical discussions about satire were of lesser interest to comedians, but prompted other conversations. This prompted me to revisit what pragmatic AR was, the study aims, my initial hunches, theory and seeing it all as interrelated; the hunchifactuality.

I've always been critical of research that excludes lived experience, and I felt that research without listening to the voices of comedians does a disservice to research and the public perception of research (see Covitt & Anderson, 2022). One of the interesting aspects of denying my own hunch that comedians didn't identify with the word satire, was my insistence upon using it. I was still used the term to give me credibility as a researcher as someone with insider positionality. This would prove to only be counterproductive, and I would have to readapt my whole approach. My own experience with this project is proof that while critics of AR claim it lacks objectivity, research for research's sake within only the theoretical boundary of a definition of satire is hardly rigorous if the participants no longer consider it relevant (Friedman & Rogers, 2009).

This also reminded me of the reason for selecting AR for my research, which was to include an intersectional[6] and decolonising[7]

---

6   This research uses the word intersectional in relation to the diversity at the intersections of satirist experiences and/or perceptions of inclusion or exclusion as related to a range of marginalised experiences; disability, race, gender, class, and other categories, framed within the power relationships of the comedy production as both systemic inequity and as a societal arena (Anthias, 2013; see also McCall, 2005). The use of the word marginalised is considered relative to

ethic; and in effect, I had to redesign the AR strategy (see figures 2 and 3 for detail of changes). Recruiting using theoretical ideas of satire wasn't needed, this was my anxiety about disciplinary boundaries and credibility. Rather than broadly use the word satire, the intended and more decolonising position would have been to draw from humour studies that challenged the traditional research paradigm. Instead of using a definition to recruit I talked to comedians about how their work might or might not be political like stiob was (Boyer & Yurchak, 2010). Through these conversations the parameters for recruiting comedians was no longer definitions of satire but comedians whose work had overt or subvert political throughlines. This renewed recruitment approach helped attract comedians to the study such as disabled comedian Maddie Stewart, who had political positions at the core of their work, rather than an occasional political reference (see also Fox, 2017; Quirk, 2015).

For example, Maddie Stewart discusses her experiences with the National Disability Insurance Scheme (NDIS) and how it limited her human rights in terms of marriage equality[8] embedded in a show that appears less political. She tells jokes about a welfare system that offers her greater freedom and less dependence on family as carers, but only if not married. The implication is that NDIS means she can get married and not have a partner expected to care for her, but her disability pension would be removed once married. She stresses, using overidentification satire, that she could not afford to live independently without financial dependence on a

---

the decolonising ethics argument of Tuhiwai Smith (2021, p. 260) in 'choosing the margins' the researcher can not only honour the struggle but also the richness and survival of those communities central to the research effort.

7 Action research has beginnings in decolonising methodological movements, and it is often considered a more ethical approach, aiming to acknowledge knowledge systems displaced by processes of colonialism and settler-colonial relationships, such as those between Indigenous nations and colonising nations (Lenette, 2022; see also Tuhiwai Smith, 2021, p. 261).

8 See https://www.abc.net.au/religion/watch/compass/marriage-equality-for-people-with-disability/103123418.

Action Research Cycle	Learning Arenas/Objectives		Analysis/synthesis questions
Plan – recruit Observe- shows of participants. Act – Interviews and satire experiments.	Recruitment done by email and Facebook in February. Observation during Melbourne International Comedy Festival in March.		
	EI round 1	Expert interviews (EI) x 3 – 6	In person interviews and observations with participants in March 2022 to July 2022
	EE round 1	March – July 2022	Ethnographic Events (EE – Satire experiments) x 1 - 2 (up to 3 participants each) conducted on campus with select audiences.
Threshold question: What themes are emerging to continue with the inquiry?			
Reflect	EI/EE follow up.	June/July/ August	Email presentation of findings and themes and offer the opportunity for comment (by phone or email or in person).
		October 2022 – January 2023	Synthesis of data –Presentation of collective ideas to community of participants.

Figure 2. The original plan, one AR cycle, two methods (participants recruited before MICF).

First AR CYCLE - Melbourne International Comedy Festival (MICF)			
AR Moments	AR Techniques (methods)		Data collection	Ongoing memo production and emergent research category coding (Charmaz, 2014)
Plan (1) - Act	Feb 2022	Scholarly input	Scholarly feedback	Action research methodology presented to 28th Australasian Humour Studies Network Conference - University of Tasmania (1)
	March - May 2022	Observation at MICF 2022 – Recruitment at MICF	Field notes, reflexive memos	Develop better understanding of comedian reticence to be known as satirists and adjusted pragmatic AR strategy (1)
Act (2) - Observe (3)		9 x expert interviews	Problem centred expert interview	3 practice-based question expert interviews delivered through the didactic method (2). Ongoing theming of data into emergent categories (3)
Act (2) Observe (3)	Apr 2022	1 x satire experiment	Political character workshop (2)	3-hour satire experiment with inexperienced practitioners (3) including 30-minute performance with a select audience
Reflect (4)	Apr – May 2022	Memos, video, transcripts, and comedian reflections		1. Close reading of data <u>initial coding</u> to develop thematic research categories 2. <u>Focused issues-based coding</u> using categories at #1.

	2nd AR Cycle - Melbourne Fringe Festival (MFF) - Shift to Eight AR Moments	
Plan (1/8)	May – Aug 2022	Expert interviews, autoethnography	**Shift to Eight AR moments to look for more categories and codes for analysis.** Review of memos and video and transcripts to shape 2nd cycle (Charmaz, 2014, 2021)
New Action (2/8)	May 2022	1 x satire experiment	3-hour satire experiment with experienced practitioners of political character comedy (30-minute performance)
Old Action Review (3/8)	June 2022 - Feb 2023	20 x expert interviews, autoethnography	Further development of research categories and emerging codes from the previous interview rounds and commence script writing for autoethnography
Observe (4/8) - Values (5/8)	Sept – Dec 2022	Autoethnography – MFF 2022	Writing, production, and development of overidentification comedy work - *Gold Star Failure* (4/8). Documentation of moderation in my work with and increased nature of political content. Peer producer and director led production (5/8).
Reflect (6/8)			All data review and reflect participants informed on a case-by-case basis regarding personalised quotes or relevant usage.
Theorise (7/8)			Qualitative coding based upon constructivist grounded theory
Conclude (8/8)			Final write-up and refinement of argument, case studies and use of participant data (with permission).

Figure 3. The final two cycle pragmatic AR model (ongoing participant recruitment).

marriage partner. She uses the irony in this situation as not in keeping with the stated goals of the NDIS, as it was meant to afford 'choice and control'. Throughout the comedy performance she evokes the irony of this system to factually critique a government system using humorous delivery. Several of the study participants used their own lived experience to critique government policy through comedy.

Had I just talked to Maddie about satire, with the original recruiting approach, she would not have seen the study as relevant to her comedy. This experience was an example of how good action research design can bridge gaps between theory and practice, even if unintentionally (Friedman & Rogers, 2009). The theory was still relevant, just not in the way I had first thought. What the cohort of comedians I worked with do, is produce comedy evoking emotive responses that meet Phiddian's (2020, p. 4) argument that satire is

> a mode rather than a genre, an aspect of some texts which allows for the expression of hostile attitudes and emotions towards figures, practices, and institutions of public significance.

My hunch about resistance to the word satire and theory about how overidentification is used in practice had come together (hunchifactually).

This prompted a pragmatic redesign three months into a planned twelve-month fieldwork project. This wasn't lost time, but better use of time, even though I struggled to imagine it as part of the process of discovery. The failed and text-based recruitment attempts forced me to get back out in the physical spaces of comedy (through festivals) and be practice and comedian oriented.

There is an irony here in that I learned that while the larrikin model of mainstream comedy can be political at times; the more contemporary larrikin performers stayed true to the larrikin history of anti-authoritarianism by not identifying as satirists. Through these conversations they also identified to me other comedians who did more deliberately subversive political content. I found the right people for my study, accidently on purpose.

All this concern with bias forced a practical rethink of my positionality as not a continuum but more of a spectrum. I was both an insider and an outsider in comedy and anthropological terms, as my comedy is outside the larrikin model, in that of the retelling of firsthand LGTBQIA+ and disability experiences made political (Krefting, 2014). The initial failures in recruitment helped me understanding this, true to Haugerud's (2013) reminders that the comedy research context is also unique as

> an anthropologist who writes about irony may as well include ironies of her [sic] ethnographic position within that frame. At first, that appears easy in this case, partly because my ethnographic interlocutors are adept at making jokes that reverse the observer-observed relation (Haugerud, 2013, p. 36).

As Haugerud (2013) notes, examining the work of those who artistically dissect societal narratives for a living is complex and is made even more complex for me by what was a dual and shifting insider and outsider positionality.

Action research aims to alleviate the tension and the power dynamics of the researcher and the researched but can create a similar paradox to that described by phenomenology (Greenwood 2002). That paradox relates to the very presence of the researcher problematically altering research outcomes if bias is not addressed (Ariel, Friedman & Agbaria, 2009; Greenwood, 2002). Good action research is designed to work explicitly with the paradox of participation to allow for documenting of hunches, any biases, and act to preserve participant experiences (the hunch factuality) without detriment to rigour or validity (Ariel et al., 2009; Greenwood, 2002; Friedman & Rogers, 2009).

This series of reflections I describe here became even clearer about halfway through what would be 16 months of fieldwork (instead of the planned 12). As I started to type up fieldworks and look for research intersections with other research, I became suddenly aware of the positionality of crossing disciplinary boundaries between anthropology and political science. I was overcompensating in my efforts to appear more objective to the critics of action research and to overcome the paradox of participation (Greenwood, 2002; Arieli et al., 2009), and failed to build participant relationships at first. This was an increased effort to maintain validity and rigour expected in political science. Validating my choice of AR through a political science lens contributed to the unconscious bias of the recruitment failures. My positionality wasn't the only issue; I was biased toward focussing on an iterative and rigorous structure to support an ethnography, when some methods were ethnographic, but it wasn't an ethnography.

Another failing of the original recruitment method was not only the issues with recruitment, but a lack of participant diversity because it looked to, predominantly, text based methods of recruitment.[9] My original design positioned recruitment efforts before the annual Melbourne International Comedy Festival (MICF), and I had planned to interview pre-selected comedians based on finding shows searched from the program with politics or satire in the show descriptions. It also failed to think in terms of the pragmatics of multiple locations. A search using the online 2022 MICF program of 502 shows with 1809 artists in 147 venues spread over 26 days in a 100 km^2 area (Melbourne International Comedy Festival, 2022, p. 1) revealed only five shows with any reference to politics and/or satire. The failure to find shows marketed as satire further proved the hunch that marginalised comedians may not always market their work as political or satire.

---

9 The use of the word diversity is defined by an intersectional framing to approach diversity as described by Anthias (2013), as a range of experiences within and between the societal arenas related to the distribution of social power. This is not just engaging with the layers of identity that form the intersections of identity, but by examining the ways the layers of those intersections are disproportionately impacted by the systems of power through issues of access to employment, or experiences such as violence and discrimination.

The issues with participant recruitment demonstrate the interconnectedness of theory, practice and lived experience. My hunch as dual insider and outsider was confirmed when comedians were not as inclined to discuss the politics of what they do publicly, by rejected a study that called them satirists. A further demonstration of this is that one participant said to me before they were interviewed, words to the effect of "yes, it's political, but can't it also just be funny?" I would then talk about my theoretical bias and how I had to unpack that, and it put comedians at ease.

I realised that I needed to be able to approach AR and hold theory, practice and lived experience together, and the redesign to pragmatic AR provided a different intent. To do this, I drew on the constructivist grounded theory approach from the work of Kathy Charmaz (2014, 2021) and her work with people with the lived experience of chronic illness (which she also had lived experience of). There might not have been a hospital to go work with patients and then recruit people later, but there were festivals. I took the approach of qualitative coding through the memo writing that Charmaz (2021) used to ensure participants' experiences were centred. Halfway through the year that followed the redesign in approach I shared my work with Dr Ogawa and his response was "you had forgotten that you are doing *pragmatic* action research."

Pragmatic Action Research is Not Just Another Method, It's a Whole System

The renewed and more pragmatic recruitment drive focussed on festivals that were the mainstay of comedian activities throughout the year instead of prioritising my methods or definitions of satire. This reworked AR strategy was successful in getting to implicit knowledge of self-censorship through the observation of reflection-in-action in satire experiments[10] and reflection-on-action through

---

10 The satire experiments involved three comedians getting into political characters (such as fictional billionaires or politicians) and performing an ad hoc TV talk show for a university audience. Performers were asked to quickly design their performance as a group in an hour before the 30-minute

problem-based expert interviews[11]. The pragmatic AR focus on festivals allowed two cycles around two festivals as well as two festival contexts (one a comedy-only festival and one a festival that included other art forms).

My original one-cycle *plan-act-observe-reflect* AR design allowed for both individual problem-based interviews and group satire experiments to observe similarities and/or differences between solo and group contexts; based on the text-based recruitment before observation and interviews. This prioritised the consecutive delivery of methods after recruitment, which was methods-centric not participant or practice led. Once I had shifted to a more genuinely pragmatic design that incorporated observation and recruitment together at festival events, ongoing recruitment allowed a focus on comedian practice that freed up time and allowed a second AR cycle to emerge.

Rather than centre comedian practices (whether hunches or not) and experience, I had centred methods not people. For example, expert interviews highlight individual decision-making of the kind that comedians do when performing solo were to be followed by group satire experiments. The satire experiments, measure comedian self-censorship when performing as a group on the same topic. This emulates what is known as a 'line-up' performance, or a group of comedians performing at an event that may not have worked together prior. Rolling out these methods in consecutive order after initial recruitment over one '(recruit) *plan* (observation of comedian shows) -*act* (interview) -*observe* (satire experiments) -

---

performance and critique current Australian political controversies for their comedic material. After the performance they would provide individual and group reflections on the experience. These events allowed the comedians to stretch the boundaries of what content and reflect on how the format impacted any self-censorship and/or content moderation.

11 Problem based expert interviews (Döringer, 2020) were didactic interviews asking comedians three questions about 1) influences on their comedy production 2) changes to how audiences received political content over the duration of their careers 3) the logic of how they moderated or self-censored (or didn't moderate or self-censor) their political content.

reflect (seek feedback)' cycle would have left little time for reflection and would make further demands on a comedian's time. By not using the same group of participants recruited at the beginning of the study, the satire experiments included people who hadn't been interviewed and didn't know each other, meaning they didn't have preconceived ideas of what was expected. This staggered and ongoing recruitment meant the satire experiments were a more organic experience, much like how a comedy line up is run in practice.

This shift in focus to festival events moved my work from the appearance of being theory heavy to look at comedian intent and it increased community interest in my research; the revised AR design became a system instead of a linear roll out of methods. The festivals became relationship-building and recruitment strategies and ways to collaboratively plan with comedians without being available 24 hours 7 days a week, in any number of comedy clubs and locations. They combined the act of observation of shows and informal chats with comedians. These chats were not limited to the participants who signed up for interviews or experiments; while I cannot ethically use that data directly, those conversations helped me gain context and insight into the broader politics of the scene (see also similar approaches by Fox, 2017 and Keisalo, 2018).

When I made the pragmatic decision to include Melbourne Fringe Festival (MFF) as well MICF, using ongoing participant recruitment (see figure 3), the festival-focus allowed better layering of the methods into two shorter pragmatic AR cycles (including enough time for the addition of a third method)[12]. The pragmatism of focusing on ongoing recruitment over two annual festivals and spending longer in relationship building and informal observation (see figure 3) increased meaningful participation in the study. This

---

12 This prompted the addition of a third method, which might seem contradictory to saving time, in an additional autoethnography as a final reflexive exercise. This autoethnography was to put on a festival show 9 months into fieldwork in a festival in my performance capacity and it further built credibility with the comedy community as they knew I was programmed to do this later in the year.

shift helped with the needed word of mouth about the research, and became vital to attracting comedians during the festival, rather than condensing recruitment in the lead up to MICF only (figure 2). Even though most comedians might be excited about an opportunity to talk about their work regardless of the time of the year; my interest in their work had to have value to their use of time and comedic priorities.

This redesigned pragmatic approach looked more like a layering of methods through a focus on festivals rather than a linear roll-out of methods. My error was holding true to traditional research methodology about recruiting *first*, instead of focussing on *participants* and *action*. Once I was able to concentrate on talking about satire in more practical terms in the field (as related to criticism of government through personal storytelling for example) engaged and interested participants agreed to be interviewed. Part of this seems obvious now, but it wasn't at time. This shift in how I presented the study and my physical presence at MICF and MFF demonstrated to participants that I was 'doing' and not only 'theorising.'

After the failed start at participant recruitment and working through my theoretical and positionality biases, I found time for two cycles of AR and decided to add an autoethnography as another method. The autoethnography took all the learnings from the previous year and put them into my own production in the 2022 Melbourne Fringe Festival (MFF)[13] as a final reflexive exercise. Melbourne Fringe Festival is conducted between September and October every year, but it is not entirely comedy like MICF. So, the inclusion of MFF also represented differing festival contexts for the performance of comedy. The decision to add another festival context, one AR cycle (associated with MICF)

---

13 The annual Melbourne Fringe Festival began in 1982 as a grassroots festival designed to further the idea of the democratisation of the arts and was open to any performer, considered a radically democratic resistance to ideas of high art and is art 'for the people, by the people' (Abrahams, Bailey, Duldig and Rhodes, 2022; Milne, 2004). Unlike MICF (which is held in March) it is not only comedic work that is presented at MFF. MFF is typically held in October.

to two festivals and two pragmatic AR cycles (the addition of MFF) allowed a shift in focus on festivals, rather than methods.

Putting participants' experiences and time first reinforces relationships before inquiry (Arieli et al., 2009). This is important when there are time challenges for a diffuse group of comedians all competing for audiences in a festival. The MFF attracts a more diverse cohort of participants in terms of comedy genre, form, style, and the personal diversity of comedians as there is less emphasis on stand-up comedy. The resultant cohort from both festival-based cycles included several intersections of personal identity from ethnic, gender, religious, class and age perspectives. The pragmatic approach harnessed the power of comedian networks from the context of MICF to MFF more efficiently. It's interesting to compare this to the initial recruitment approach of using social media groups to attract participants. When I shared social media assets advertising the study in social media groups (with hundreds of comedians as members) referring to the study in terms of satire definitions, I only got one interested comedian, who later declined to be interviewed.

That initial insider hunch about comedians avoiding political marketing did not need to be ignored entirely as potential bias, I could have listened to it more and it highlights how much 'doing research' changes the dynamics of everyday experience. The pragmatic focus on festivals and different performance contexts also helped delineate differences and similarities in mainstream and grassroots comedian experiences. This festival focus also was a measure relevant to a minimum expectation of festival experience for producing solo shows at the grassroots level to be able to access national TV, radio, publishing, and podcast career trajectories.

Good participatory theory does not seek cause and effect between comedian and politics; but instead seeks to understand the experiences of participants engaged in the complex human process of making meaning through the comedy of lived experience. Good action science as Friedman & Rogers (2009) describes, unearths the meanings participants give to their actions to examine power relationships that can be used to predict behaviour. In this case, the rich data of the interviews pointed to several techniques to enhance political expression through subtler comedic means as well as sociopolitical and socioeconomic barriers to that freedom of expression. Friedman and Rogers (2009) describe this type of knowledge production as 'theories of action' or 'action science'. So, this project produces knowledge about comedians and their 'theories-in-use' as the action science of the politics of their decision-making while recognising them as the producers of comedy.

A key question of this research was related to whether Australian comedy had the subversive status quo-shifting satirical techniques described by Boyer and Yurchak (2010) in the post-Soviet era and the United States. The pragmatic AR approach brought both more and less structure to comedic chaos, which led to a better understanding of the how and the why of when comedians were shying away from the label of satire. A range of intersections of marginalised personal identities was represented in the grassroots sample and the best way I can describe this happening was that it 'just sort of fell out of the data collection process.' This also helped to understand similarities and differences in experiences related to the politics of identity and oppression and how they drive comedy as acts of persistence and resistance (even if unintentionally at times). It was hoped that around three mainstream and six grassroots comedians would participate, but the pragmatic approach resulted in a higher-than-expected response rate of 29 interviews (approximately 30% mainstream and 70% grassroots). As well as human diversity the adapted pragmatic AR strategy found a more diverse range of the target satire/political comedy than expected, more 'hiding in plain sight' overidentification comedy in the Australian context.

This highlighted some contrasting and similar experiences of grassroots and mainstream performers. Most of the initial cycle was grassroots comedians (eight out of nine interviewed) and one mainstream comedian with extensive satire production experience. I wanted to make sure I wasn't reifying patterns in that data with only grassroots experiences for the next round of interviews. By moving into another round of recruitment, I could talk about the first cycle with potential participants, and this allowed me to attract higher-profile mainstream comedians to the second cycle. The additional cycle allowed for this nuance that can prevent a common researcher pitfall in

> conventional social science…get[ting] stuck in observing and analysing without easily moving on to planning and action-or alternatively may get stuck in experimental action without easily incorporating the relevant field-based generation of that theory (Wadsworth, 2014, p. 33).

A pragmatic AR approach, focussed on how comedians were organised relative to what was important to them, meant further centring comedian experiences, processes, and logic, rather than the imposition of methods upon participants.

In working to position comedians' lived experience alongside the time pressures of the festival season, the pragmatic AR strategy (figure 3) streamlined communication, so it became about a collegiate exchange of expertise at both research and peer levels. This approach

> combines two seemingly contradictory sources of knowledge, as it gives equal right to the previously accumulated theoretical and empirical knowledge of the researcher and the individual knowledge and personal experiences of the respondent (Döringer, 2020, p. 4).

In the interview space, a conversational problem-based interviewing style based on three questions drew out underpinning knowledge (Döringer, 2020) while safely examining the influence of accepted comedy production norms.

The pragmatic approach did not mean that the delivery of methods or theory were not important, or that the *Plan-Act-Observe-Reflect* structure was fundamentally different, just more practice-focused. Traditional research thinking was still adopted albeit applied through the lens of participant experience and in doing so, festival time was leveraged, not cheated. This renewed AR research design with ongoing recruitment produced rich data about how and why comedians moderate or self-censor and moderate political content. This data was relevant to the political environment and not solely comedian technique.[14] Most of the time comedians are involved in research they are asked about their techniques and how they write comedy, not what they leave out or why. The research design uncovered underpinning knowledge for several participants as they expressed how their decision-making worked through the expression of "ah-ha…that's related to" scenarios. Had I stuck with a linear rollout of methods, one cycle and continued to recruit comedians based on notions of satire without fully examining my biases, I doubt any of this would have been possible nor would the data be as nuanced.

Conclusion

This pragmatic AR strategy, temporally attached to comedian-led festival practice produced rich data revealing insights into comedian agency as they navigate issues like self-censorship in the Australian socio-political context. As someone who both needs structure but loves discovery, I found myself considering a career counting bird eggs in some remote place. However, as I was there with comedians harnessing the changing and flexible process of this research and tying it to their practice it facilitated unlearning and co-learning. This research process of unlearning my traditional research bias was part of a co-learning process, alongside comedians as they unpacked how they adjust to the changing environment of Australian comedy production.

I feel very privileged to share a hunchifactuality with comedians who work to make the world a better place through the humanity of laughter. There is an irony within studying irony here; if I continued to recruit comedians based on the explicitly theoretical

---

14 Just prior to interview and satire experiments, comedians were reminded that the PhD was aimed at political influences, not a deconstruction of techniques they used. There was some cross over in these discussions as some techniques are political by nature, for example, using absurdity to critique a politician to avoid defamation or censorship. However, this emphasis on political influences

on their work in terms of marginalisation, economics, government funding and national identity was an effective delimiter to interviews and satire experiments.

and traditional approach pretending to be AR, I would have failed to find the 'hiding in plain sight' comedy of this study. This rich data gleaned from the process of a pragmatic AR approach presents a clear demonstration of the power of the subversive comedy measures in what can be a hostile place for marginalised comedians. Contrary to the criticisms of subjectivity place upon AR and for those with insider experiences, it was my attempts to be objective that led to the need for a more effective AR redesign. Instead, a pragmatic AR strategy focusing back on the *comedian's meaning making*, alleviated bias and achieved a more holistic recruitment of participants.

References

Abrahams, S., Bailey, J., Duldig, P., & Rhodes, K. (2022) *The rest is up to you, Melbourne Fringe Festival 1982 - 2062; A book about the past, present and future of Melbourne Fringe*. State Library of Victoria.

Anthias, F. (2013) Intersectional what? Social divisions, intersectionality, and levels of analysis. *Ethnicities*. 13 (1). https://doi.org/10.1177/1468796812463547.

Arieli, D., Friedman, V. J., & Agbaria, K. (2009) The paradox of participation in action research. *Action Research*. 7 (3), https://doi.org/10.1177/1476750309336718.

Brookfield, J. (2019) *No apologies: Women in comedy, claiming their space, finding their voices, and telling their stories*. London, Echo Publishing.

Bogad, L.M (2005) Electoral guerrilla theatre in Australia: Pauline Hanson vs. Pauline Pantsdown. In: Bogad, L.M. *Electoral guerrilla theatre, radical ridicule and social movements*. Routledge, pp. 165-201.

Boyer, D. & Yurchak, A. (2010) American Stiob: Or what late-socialist aesthetics of parody reveal about contemporary political culture in the West. *Cultural Anthropology*. 25 (2), 179–221.

Brewis, J. (2014) The ethics of researching friends: On convenience sampling in qualitative management and organization studies. *British Journal of Management*. 25 (4), 849–862. https://doi.org/10.1111/1467-8551.12064.

Charmaz, K. (2014) *Constructing grounded theory*. SAGE.

Charmaz, K. (2021) The genesis, grounds, and growth of constructivist grounded theory. In: Morse, J. M., Bowers, B. J., Charmaz, K., Clarke, A. E., Corbin, J., Porr, C. J. & Stern, P. N. (eds.) *Developing grounded theory*. Routledge. pp. 153–187. https://doi.org/10.4324/9781315169170.

Condren, C. (2012) Satire and definition. *Humor*. 25 (4), 375-399. https://doi.org/10.1515/humor-2012-0019.

Cook, P., & Heilmann, C. (2013) Two types of self-censorship: Public and private. *Political Studies*. 61 (1), 178-196. https://doi.org/10.1111/j.1467-9248.2012.00957.x

Cothren, A., & Phiddian, R. (2019, March 14). Friday essay: why is Australian satire so rarely risky? *The Conversation*. http://theconversation.com/friday-essay-why-is-australian-satire-so-rarely-risky-112689.

Covitt, B.A. & Anderson, C.W. (2022) Untangling trustworthiness and uncertainty in science. *Science & Education*. 31, 1155–1180. https://doi.org/10.1007/s11191-022-00322-6.

Dawson, A. & Brady, J. (2021, July 28) The policing of Australian satire: why defamation is still no joke, despite recent law changes. *The Conversation*. https://theconversation.com/the-policing-of-australian-satire-why-defamation-is-still-no-joke-despite-recent-law-changes-164076.

Day, A. (2011) *Satire and dissent: Interventions in contemporary political debate*. Indiana University Press.

Döringer, S. (2020) The problem-centred expert interview. Combining qualitative interviewing approaches for investigating implicit expert knowledge. *International Journal of Social Research Methodology*. 24 May. https://doi.10.1080/13645579.2020.1766777.

Fox, K. E. (2017) *Stand up and be (en) countered: Resistance in solo stand-up performance by Northern English women marginalised on the basis of gender, class, and regional identity*. University of Leeds.

Fox, K. (2018) Humitas: Humour as performative resistance. In: MacKenzie, I., Francis, F., & Giappone, K. B. R. (eds.). *Comedy and critical thought: Laughter as resistance*. Rowman & Littlefield Unlimited Model.

Friedman, V. J., & Rogers, T. (2009) There is nothing so theoretical as good action research. *Action Research*, 7 (1), 31–47. https://doi.org/10.1177/1476750308099596.

Greenwood, D.J. (2002) Action research: Unfulfilled promises and unmet challenges. *Concepts and Transformations* 7 (2), 117-139.

Greenwood, D. J. (2007) Pragmatic action research. *International Journal of Action Research*, 3 (1+2), 131-148. https://nbn-resolving.org/urn:nbn:de:0168-ssoar-412899.

Greenwood, D. J. & Levin, M. (2007) *An epistemological foundation for action research*. SAGE Publications, Inc. https://dx.doi.org/10.4135/9781412984614.

Haugerud, A. (2013) *No billionaire left behind: Satirical activism in America*. Stanford University Press. http://www.sup.org/books/title/?id=21675.

Herr, K., & Anderson, G. L. (2005) *The action research dissertation: A guide for students and faculty*. SAGE Publications, Inc. https://dx.doi.org/10.4135/9781452226644.

Higgie, R. L. (2013) *Speaking truth: the play of politics and Australian satire*. Doctoral Dissertation, Curtin University, Department of Communication and Cultural Studies. https://catalogue.curtin.edu.au/permalink/f/ndovj9/cur_dspace_dc 20.500.11937/2180.

Holm, N. (2017) *Humour as politics*. Springer International Publishing. https://doi.org/10.1007/978-3-319-50950-1.

Kavanagh, D. (1991) Why political science needs history. *Political Studies*. 39, 479-495. https://doi.org/10.1111/j.1467-9248.1991.tb01624.x.

Keisalo, M. (2018) The invention of gender in stand-up comedy: transgression and digression. *Social Anthropology*. 26 (4), 550–563. https://doi.org/10.1111/1469-8676.12515.

Knowles, M. (2022) *Larrikins, listeners and lifeline: Inside Australian comedy chatcast. The little Dum Dum Club*. Master's thesis, University of Melbourne. Minerva access hdl.handle.net/11343/325207.

Krefting, R. (2014) *All joking aside: American humor and its discontents*. Johns Hopkins University Press.

Lenette, C. (2022) Why decolonize? Participatory action research's origins, decolonial research, and intersectionality. *Participatory action research: Ethics and decolonization*. New York, Oxford Academic, 19 May 2022), https://doi.org/10.1093/oso/9780197512456.003.0002.

Lin, H. (2023) Data hunches: Expressing personal knowledge in data visualizations. *Doctor of philosophy in computing*, The University of Utah.

McCall, L. (2005) The complexity of intersectionality. *Signs: Journal of Women in Culture and Society.* 30 (3). https://doi.org/10.1086/426800.

Melbourne International Comedy Festival (2022) *Melbourne International Comedy Festival 2022 Festival Report.* Melbourne, Melbourne International Comedy Festival.

Milner Davis, J. & Foyle, L. (2017) The satirist, the larrikin & the politician: An Australian perspective on satire & politics. In Milner Davis, J. (ed.) *Satire and politics: The interplay of heritage and practice.* London, Palgrave Macmillan, pp. 1-35.

Ogawa, A. (2006) Initiating change: *Doing action research in Japan. Dispatches from the field: neophyte ethnographers in a changing world.* Waveland Press, Inc. pp. 207 – 221.

Phiddian, R. (2017). Have they no shame? Observations on the effects of satire. In: *Satire and Politics: The interplay of heritage and practice.* London, Palgrave Macmillan. pp. 251–263.

Phiddian, R. (2020) *Satire and the public emotions.* Cambridge University Press.

Quirk, S. (2015) *Why stand-up matters: How comedians manipulate and influence.* Methuen Drama.

Rickard, J. (1998) Lovable larrikins and awful ockers. *Journal of Australian Studies.* 22 (56), 78–85. https://doi.org/10.1080/14443059809387362.

Sless. J. (2022) *Mistress of Mirth's Comedy Tour.* North Melbourne, Australian Scholarly Publishing.

Sparrow, A. (2024) *Humour and the appearance of authenticity in live comedy (Version 1).* Open Access Te Herenga Waka-Victoria University of Wellington. https://doi.org/10.26686/wgtn.25304839.

Throsby, D. & Petetskaya, K. (2024) *Artists as workers: An economic study of professional artists in Australia.* Department of Economics, Macquarie Business School Macquarie University.

Throsby, D., & Zednik, A. (2010) *Do you really expect to get paid? an economic study of professional artists in Australia.* Australia Council for the Arts (Creative Australia).

Tuhiwai Smith, L. (2021) Choosing the margins: The role of research in Indigenous struggles for social justice. In: *Decolonizing methodologies: Research and Indigenous Peoples.* London, Zed Books. pp. 253–272. Retrieved February 20, 2024, from http://dx.doi.org/10.5040/9781350225282.0017.

Yurchak, A. (2006) *Dead irony: Necroaesthetics, "Stiob" and the Anekdot. In Everything Was Forever, Until It Was No More.* pp. 238–281.

Wadsworth, Y. (2014) *Building in research and evaluation: Human inquiry for living systems.* Routledge.

Wadsworth, Y. (2015) Shared inquiry capabilities and differing inquiry preferences: Navigating 'full cycle' iterations of action research. In: Bradbury, H. (Ed.) *The SAGE Handbook of Action Research.* SAGE Publications Ltd. pp. 750–759.
https://doi.org/10.4135/9781473921290.

Biography

Jack Brady is an applied anthropologist and political science PhD candidate at the University of Melbourne (final year). They are a community engaged researcher specialising in the representation of marginalised community voices through pragmatic action research in community-based (non-for-profit) programs, projects and campaigns.

Photo credit: Paul Dunn

Book Review – *A 101 Action Research Guide for Beginners*

Yedida Bessemer

A 101 Action Research Guide for Beginners (2024) by Saba Ahmed is a practical book for novice action researchers, particularly in STEM (science, technology, engineering, and mathematics) education. The book's title indicates its purpose - to demystify research terminology and provide concrete examples of action research in practice. This guide opens a gate for educators and practitioners looking to engage in action research for the first time or after a significant break from academic research.

Each of the book's eight chapters focuses on a key aspect of action research. Chapter one sets the context for the rest of the book by exploring contemporary STEM teaching. Chapter two provides important tips on academic and reflective writing and essential skills for action researchers. The following two chapters, three and four, address the fundamental research terminology and introduce data collection methods. Chapter five deals with the crucial aspect of maintaining quality assurance in research projects. The author provides practical examples to help the readers better understand the transformation of theoretical concepts into real-world research. Chapters six and seven present the readers with a sample research proposal and a complete exemplar STEM lecturer action research project, respectively. Chapter eight examines the significance of developing research skills starting at the undergraduate level, emphasizing the long-term benefits of STEM practice.

Ahmed's approach of explaining complex research concepts in simple terms is particularly valuable for beginners or those returning back to research after a long break; it demystifies the research process and makes it less intimidating for novice researchers. This guide contributed to action research literature by connecting theory and practice, and it's a key strength of the book.

> All educators new to teaching will be exposed to many "…isms" (behaviourism, humanism, constructivism, cognitivism) where teachers will be confronted with unravelling how theories are consequential in course delivery, to improve the learner experience and their teaching pedagogy. Each teacher is different, and the pertinence of each learning theory will differ. Some may find humanism elements more useful, and yet others may favour constructivism (this is to be expected). Yet all teachers need to demonstrate an understanding and openness to other learning theories, because unexpectedly it could add value if not now then potentially in future practice. Teaching practice is a spectrum. By learning the foundations of each theory teachers/ lecturers can pick and choose the level and degree to which it permeates into their teaching delivery, and on how they can affect action research projects. (p. 5)

Since there is an increase in education on STEM and evidence-based practice in these STEM fields, this guide is relevant, especially now. The examples and case studies from STEM disciplines can help educators improve their instruction and learning outcomes. The author uses a practical approach that speaks to educators who want to enhance their practice through research.

Moreover, the author discusses different types of action research, such as first-person, second-person, and third-person, and framework so researchers can choose the one that aligns with their research questions. Furthermore, Ahmed integrates her explanation of action research with national and international teaching frameworks, such as the Initial Teacher Training and Early Career Framework (ITTECFT). This connection shows how action research can be integrated into professional development and practice improvement.

The book offers a holistic perspective to conducting effective action research. It thoroughly covers the research process, ranging from writing tips to data collection methods and quality assurance. By including a complete research proposal and a project report in Chapters Six and Seven, Ahmed demonstrates to the readers how all the research elements come together in a real-world context. In addition, the author stresses the importance of reflective practice and developing research skills at the undergraduate level. Ahmed advocates for integrating research skills into STEM curricula to foster a research mindset and benefit future STEM professionals.

The book provides a roadmap for educators and novice researchers who wish to develop and implement action research to help them improve their practice. It includes practical applications such as a step-by-step guide to conducting action research projects and examples, templates, and links. Moreover, it highlights reflective practice for continuing professional learning. However, since it focuses on STEM education, it may limit its applicability to researchers in other fields.

All in all, *A 101 Action Research Guide for Beginners* (2024) is an essential additional source to the action research literature, mainly for those new to the field or working in STEM education because it provides a comprehensive examination of the research process while focusing on practical application as well as its accessibility. In other words, it demystifies the action research process and its terminology for novice researchers, especially those seeking to integrate research into their professional teaching practice and develop their research skills. This guide encourages educators, especially in the STEM disciplines and beginner researchers, to explore, learn, and apply the knowledge and skills provided in this book to enhance their practice through purposeful research.

References

Ahmed, S. (2024) *A 101 action research guide for beginners: Demystifying action research terminology using a concrete STEM action research project*. Oxford, UK, Peter Lang Ltd.

Membership information and article submissions

Membership categories

Membership of Action Learning, Action Research Association Ltd (ALARA) takes two forms: individual and organisational.

ALARA individual membership

Members of the ALARA obtain access to all issues of the *Action Learning and Action Research Journal* (*ALARj*) twelve months before it becomes available to the public.

ALARA members receive regular emailed Action Learning and Action Research updates and access to web-based networks, discounts on conference/seminar registrations, and an on-line membership directory. The directory has details of members with information about interests as well as the ability to contact them.

ALARA organisational membership

ALARA is keen to make connections between people and activities in all strands, streams and variants associated with our paradigm. Areas include Action Learning, Action Research, process management, collaborative inquiry facilitation, systems thinking, Indigenous research and organisational learning and development. ALARA may appeal to people working at all levels in any kind of organisational, community, workplace or other practice setting.

ALARA invites organisational memberships with university schools, public sector units, corporate and Medium to Small Business, and community organisations. Such memberships include Affiliates. Details are on our membership link on our website (https://alarassociation.org/membership/Affiliates).

Become a member of ALARA

An individual Membership Application Form is on the last page of this Journal or individuals can join by clicking on the Membership Application button on ALARA's website. Organisations can apply by using the organisational membership application form on ALARA's website.

> ## For more information on ALARA activities and to join
> Please visit our web page:
> https://www.alarassociation.org/user/register
> or email admin@alarassociation.org

Journal submissions criteria and review process

The *ALARj* contains substantial articles, project reports, information about activities, creative works from the Action Learning and Action Research field, reflections on seminars and conferences, short articles related to the theory and practice of Action Learning and Action Research, and reviews of recent publications. *ALARj* also advertises practitioners' services for a fee.

The *ALARj* aims to be of the highest standard of writing from the field in order to extend the boundaries of theorisation of the practice, as well as the boundaries of its application.

ALARA aims *ALARj* to be accessible for readers and contributors while not compromising the need for sophistication that complex situations require. We encourage experienced practitioners and scholars to contribute, while being willing to publish new practitioners as a way of developing the field, and introduce novice practitioners presenting creative and insightful work

We will only receive articles that have been proof read, comply with the submission guidelines as identified on *ALARj*'s website, and that meet the criteria that the reviewers use. We are unlikely to publish an article that describes a project simply because its methodology is drawn from our field.

ALARA intends *AlARj* to provide high quality works for practitioners and funding bodies to use in the commissioning of works, and the progression of and inclusion of action research and action learning concepts and practices in policy and operations.

ALARj has a substantial international panel of experienced Action Learning and Action Research scholars and practitioners who offer double blind and transparent reviews at the request of the author.

Making your submission and developing your paper

Please send all contributions in Microsoft Word format to the Open Journal Systems (OJS) access portal: https://alarj.alarassociation.org.

You must register as an author to upload your document and work through the electronic pages of requirements to make your submission. ALARA's Managing Editor or Issue Editor will contact you and you can track progress of your paper on the OJS page.

If you have any difficulties or inquiries about submission or any other matters to do with ALARA publications contact the Managing Editor on editor@alarassociation.org.

For the full details of submitting to the *ALAR Journal*, please see the submission guidelines on ALARA's web site https://alarassociation.org/publications/submission-guidelines/alarj-submission-guidelines.

Guidelines

ALARj is devoted to the communication of the theory and practice of Action Learning, Action Research and related methodologies generally. As with all ALARA activities, all streams of work across all disciplines are welcome. These areas include Action Learning, Action Research, Participatory Action Research, systems thinking, inquiry process-facilitation, process management, and all the associated post-modern epistemologies and methods such as rural self-appraisal, auto-ethnography, appreciative inquiry, most significant change, open space technology, etc.

In reviewing submitted papers, our reviewers use the following criteria, which are important for authors to consider:

Criterion 1: How well are the paper and its focus both aimed at and/or grounded in the world of practice?

Criterion 2: How well are the paper and/or its subject explicitly and actively participative: research with, for and by people rather than on people?

Criterion 3: How well do the paper and/or its subject draw on a wide range of ways of knowing (including intuitive, experiential, presentational as well as conceptual) and link these appropriately to form theory of and in practices (praxis)?

Criterion 4: How well does the paper address questions that are of significance to the flourishing of human community and the more-than-human world as related to the foreseeable future?

Criterion 5: How well does the paper consider the ethics of research practice for this and multiple generations?

Criterion 6: How well does the paper and/or its subject aim to leave some lasting capacity amongst those involved, encompassing first, second and third person perspectives?

Criterion 7: How well do the paper and its subject offer critical insights into and critical reflections on the research and inquiry process?

Criteria 8: How well does the paper openly acknowledge there are culturally distinctive approaches to Action Research and Action Learning and seek to make explicit their own assumptions about non-Western/ Indigenous and Western approaches to Action Research and Action Learning

Criteria 9: How well does the paper engage the context of research with systemic thinking and practices

Criterion 10: How well do the paper and/or its subject progress AR and AL in the field (research, community, business, education or otherwise)?

Criterion 11: How well is the paper written?

Article preparation

ALARj submissions must be original and unpublished work suitable for an international audience and not under review by any other publisher or journal. No payment is associated with submissions. Copyright of published works remains with the author(s) shared with Action Learning, Action Research Association Ltd

While *ALARj* promotes established practice and related discourse *ALARj* also encourages unconventional approaches to reflecting on practice including poetry, artworks and other forms of creative expression that can in some instances progress the field more appropriately than academic forms of writing.

Submissions are uploaded to our Open Journal System (OJS) editing and publication site.

The reviewers use the OJS system to send authors feedback within a 2-3 month period. You will receive emails at each stage of the process with feedback, and if needed, instructions included in the email about how to make revisions and resubmit.

Access to the journal

The journal is published electronically on the OJS website.

EBSCO and InformIT also publish the journal commercially for worldwide access, and pdf or printed versions are available from various online booksellers or email admin@alarassociation.org.

For further information about the *ALAR Journal* and other ALARA publications, please see ALARA's web site http://www.alarassociation.org/publications.

Individual Membership Application Form

This form is for the use of individuals wishing to join ALARA.
Please complete all fields.

Name
Title	Given Name		Family Name

Residential Address
Street		Town / City	Postcode / Zip
Country			

Postal Address
Street		Town / City	Postcode / Zip
State	Country		

Telephone
Country Code	Telephone Number

Mobile Telephone
Country Code	Mobile Number

Email
Email Address

Experience (Please tick most relevant)
- [ ] No experience yet
- [ ] 1 – 5 years' experience
- [ ] More than 5 years' experience

Interests (Please tick all relevant)
- [ ] Education
- [ ] Health
- [ ] Community / Social Justice
- [ ] Indigenous Issues
- [ ] Gender Issues
- [ ] Organizational Development

Are you eligible for concessional membership?
If you are a full-time student, retired or an individual earning less than AUD 20,000 per year, about USD 13,750 (please check current conversion rates), you can apply for concessional membership.

Do you belong to an organization that is an Organizational Member of ALARA?
If you are a member of such an organization, you can apply for the Reduced Membership Fee. Please state the name of the Organizational Member of ALARA in the box below.

Annual Membership Fees (Please select one)

Full Membership		Concessional Membership	
AUD 143.00	Developed Country	AUD 71.50	
AUD 99.00	Emerging Country	AUD 49.50	
AUD 55.00	Developing Country	AUD 27.50	

Reduced Membership Fee, as I belong to an Organizational Member of ALARA	Developed	AUD 71.50
	Emerging	AUD 49.50
	Developing	AUD 27.50

Organization's name: _____

Payment
We offer a range of payment options. Details are provided on the Tax Invoice that we will send to you on receipt of your membership application.

If you want to join and pay online, please go to https://www.alarassociation.org and click on the Membership Application button (lower right). Alternatively, please complete and return this form to us.

By Post
ALARA Membership
PO Box 162 Greenslopes
Queensland 4120
AUSTRALIA

By FAX
+ 61 (7) 3342 1669

By Email
admin@alarassociation.org

Privacy Policy
By submitting this membership form, I acknowledge that I have read, understood and accept ALARA's Privacy Policy
https://www.alarassociation.org/sites/default/files/docs/policies/ALARA_PrivacyPolicy11_1.pdf

ALARA will acknowledge receipt of your application and send you an invoice or receipt of payment. You will receive an email confirming activation of your account, and details on how you can access website functions.

Printed by Libri Plureos GmbH in Hamburg, Germany